From Calcutta to Connecticut

An Intern's Tale of Two Cultures

Amitabha Ghosh Roy, M.D.

From Calcutta to Connecticut, published April, 2021

Editorial & Proofreading: Kathleen A. Tracy, Karen Grennan
Cover Design: Howard Johnson
Interior Design & Layout: Howard Johnson
Images: *Cover images:* Calcutta Hospital: Varley II John - Medical College Hospital Calcutta - British School - 19th Century, Alamy Stock Photo; Image ID:2CFN3E4; Griffin Hospital: "Vintage Early 1900's Postcard - Griffin Hospital, Derby, CT" Pintrest
Title page: Old Compass on Vintage Map Creator: tonefotografia;
Chapter openers: Mandella, Designed by Visnezh / Freepik; Getty Images/iStockphoto, Copyright: tonefotografia
Photo credits: Photos on pages 197 and 198 owned by Amitabha Ghosh Roy, M.D.

Published by SDP Publishing, an imprint of SDP Publishing Solutions, LLC.
For more information about this book, contact Lisa Akoury-Ross at SDP Publishing by email at info@SDPPublishing.com.

All rights reserved. No part of the material protected by this copyright notice may be reproduced or utilized in any form or by any means, electronic or mechanical, including photocopying, recording, or by any information storage and retrieval system, without written permission from the copyright owner.

To obtain permission(s) to use material from this work, please submit a written request to:

SDP Publishing
Permissions Department
PO Box 26
East Bridgewater, MA 02333
or email your request to info@SDPPublishing.com

ISBN-13 (paperback): 978-1-7361990-7-7
ISBN-13 (hardcover) 978-1-7361990-8-4
ISBN-13 (ebook): 978-1-7361990-9-1

Printed in the United States of America

Copyright 2021 © Amitabha Ghosh Roy, M.D.

Dedication

I dedicate this book and make my pranam *to my revered parents, Jitendra and Labanya, who gave me wings and allowed me to fly.*

ACKNOWLEDGMENTS

I thank my wife, Margaret, for her encouragement, patience, and enormous help with the manuscript from the very beginning.

Table of Contents

Preface 9

Introduction: The Yellow Brick Road 11

1: Colonial India 15

2: Kites, Cobras, and Cannabis 31

3: Land of Famine 49

4: Rising to the Challenges 55

5: Have Stethoscope Will Travel 69

6: Welcome to the Emerald City 91

7: Medical Culture Shock 117

8: So This is America 131

9: Homesick 145

10: Talking Turkey 153

11: Rides and Rotations 161

12: Merry and Bright . . . and Surreal 175

13: The Year Comes to an End 181

Epilogue: A Man of Two Cultures 193

Preface

I have been a physician for more than fifty years, and the idea to write a book was planted over the years by friends and colleagues who encouraged me to put pen to paper after hearing about my experiences and the difficulties I initially faced as an intern from India. While many others have shared the same medical calling and perhaps even shared similar backgrounds, the majority have not articulated their personal stories. I decided I would. And once I retired in 2012, I finally had the time to do so. It has been a slow process but a fruitful one.

I grew up in India and started medical school there in the 1950s, with dreams of being a surgeon, although I had never considered it would happen in the United States. But through a bit of serendipity, I was brought to America by a hospital in Connecticut, the Griffin Hospital in Derby, and thus began my multi-continent journey where I'd acclimate to contrasting cultural norms, adjust to radically more advanced medical technology, and grow to embrace my new surroundings while still holding my familial and emotional ties to India close.

During that internship year at the Griffin Hospital, I encountered patients and cases along the way that

I have never forgotten. Practicing medicine in India compared to what I encountered in the United States was a stark contrast of facilities, resources, and training. During that intern year I learned as much about American life as I did the wonders of advanced medical training and technology. It was a completely different culture and despite my occasional bemusement at American traditions—such as their obsession with turkey in the autumn—I was charmed by the people I met and drawn to the opportunities found here. My year as an intern turned into the springboard for my future, and my adopted country ultimately enabled me to become the surgeon I always wanted to be.

Native-born Americans tend to take their way of life and customs for granted. I hope reading about my experiences will help people appreciate the challenging learning curve those new to this country must navigate to try and fit in. From expected social niceties and showering wearing no clothes—and feeling more than naked—to the casual attire worn by most people and the local cuisine, everything was so foreign at first. But for someone coming here as I did, it was also wondrous, and the opportunities provided—education, a career, a wife, and family—were ultimately worth any moments of uncertainty, awkwardness, or embarrassment I initially experienced.

This is my story. I hope you find the journey recounted here as interesting to read about as it was to live it.

—Dr. Roy

Introduction:
The Yellow Brick Road

There are moments in our life that we never forget, that remain as vivid and emotionally impactful years after the fact. The birth of a child, the loss of a parent, the first time you set eyes on the love of your life—such defining occurrences are not just seared into your memory but your senses. One of the moments for me occurred in the early afternoon of July 16, 1962, when I landed at New York's Idlewild Airport, now known as JFK International.

After traveling for almost twenty-four hours from Calcutta on BOAC—the British Overseas Airways Corporation would later become British Airways—we disembarked into what was to me a dazzle of modern artistic design. Or as *Time* magazine would put it: "For eight of eleven international travelers presently arriving in New York, the warming symbol of journey's end no longer is the stately, green copper Statue of Liberty seen from a boat deck, but a glistening complex of low-lying architecture—strongly suggestive of a world's fair site—seen from the window of an airplane."

I followed the other passengers from my flight through

the bustling parade of arriving and departing fliers to the baggage claim. Everything was so new, so unfamiliar, and so unknown, but I felt no apprehension or anxiety, just enjoyment at being in the United States, half a world away from my native India. Going through customs and immigration was surprisingly uncomplicated and hassle-free. The immigration agent was friendly and complimented me on my good English. That was probably the last time I would have such an easy encounter with airport immigration.

I plucked my lone suitcase off the carousel—it was little more than a carry-on, containing two shirts, a pair of pants, and a few other small items—and exited baggage claim. There were signs for ground transportation as well as signs directing people where to go for connecting flights. The Griffin Hospital that had hired me as an intern was supposed to send someone to pick me up and drive me to Connecticut. But I saw nobody with a sign bearing my name. Today we'd have a phone number we could text; in 1962 all you had were payphones. And I had absolutely no idea where to go or how to contact anyone. I stood stranded in the sea of people swirling around me.

I went to the information desk; they could not help me. A fellow passenger from my plane tried to help me but had to leave when his ride showed up. At that point, an extremely helpful BOAC stewardess from my flight came to the rescue. She somehow found out that my ride was on his way and stayed with me until he arrived.

Despite having to depend on the kindness of strangers after just arriving in a far-away country where I knew nobody, had no ride, and didn't know who to contact at the hospital, I felt no anxiety, no apprehension. I was totally calm, maybe even exhilarated as I observed people of all shades coming out of the international terminal speaking unfamiliar languages, all so different from me. India is a large country, but that day at the airport was when it fully struck me just how big the world really was.

After about a half-hour wait, my ride to the hospital, who introduced himself as Mr. Kelly, finally arrived. We shook hands. Had we been in India, I would have probably said *namaskar* with folded hands. He apologized for being late, saying he couldn't find a parking space. At the time I didn't quite understand what he meant or why that would make him so late. (I would soon learn.) He asked me to wait outside by the curb while he went to get the car. The BOAC stewardess said good-bye and wished me luck. Watching her walk away I felt alone and uneasy for the first time. I wondered what would happen if Mr. Kelly did not come back for me. The hospital had never told me about Mr. Kelly. How could I be sure he was going to take me to the hospital in Connecticut where I was going to work?

As I fretted, I slowly took in my surroundings. It was a gorgeous warm and sunny day. The sky was azure blue accented with wispy, white, cotton-ball clouds floating by, propelled by a cool breeze. Most of the people who passed by—locals, not travelers—were wearing stylish colorful clothes. But I was taken aback by the young ladies who wore shorts and walked hand in hand with their friends, some of them smoking. But most shocking—I'm sure my eyes were so wide in surprise that they looked about to pop out of my head—was seeing some young women kissing their (I presumed) boyfriends or husbands out in the open in front of everyone, happy and carefree. For as scandalous as it was to me, nobody else seemed to mind the public displays of affection much.

As I was trying to absorb this absolutely unbelievable scene, Mr. Kelly came with his car and interrupted my reverie. Getting in the car I realized I wasn't in Kansas—or Calcutta—anymore.

Colonial India

I grew up in Jalpaiguri, India, a small, beautiful town—actually, more like a glorified village—nestled amongst the tea gardens in the foothills of the Himalayas in northern Bengal province. Despite our small size, my hometown enjoyed a rich culture filled with art, music, and cultural activities. Sports were also popular, especially soccer and cricket—two sports invented by the British and brought to India. We even had two soccer players from our town play in the Olympics. But these idyllic early watercolor memories belie the rising political and social tensions sweeping through the subcontinent that were part and parcel of living under British colonial rule in the 1930s and 1940s.

I was born in the summer of 1936, and the India of my childhood was a country in the midst of dramatic change, a time of uncertainty, activism, upheaval, and hope that had been centuries in the making. I grew up during the time of the British Raj, what they called Britain's colonial rule of India, which began in 1858 after control by the East India Company was transferred to the British Crown under Queen Victoria. But India's complex relationship with—and many would say subjugation by—the British began centuries earlier.

In 1600 a group of London merchants secured a royal charter from Queen Elizabeth I to trade in the East Indies. The original intent of the merchants, who named their enterprise the East India Company, was to trade for spices at islands in present-day Indonesia. Their ships set sail on the Company's first voyage in February 1601. But things didn't go as planned. The Dutch already had a strong foothold in Indonesia, so after butting heads with Dutch and Portuguese traders, the East India Company focused their entrepreneurial attention on the Indian subcontinent, which was known for its fine cotton and exotic spices such as turmeric, pepper, and ginger as well as other commodities. English traders set up outposts on the Indian coasts, which would evolve into the cities of Bombay, Madras, and Calcutta—known today as Mumbai, Chennai, and Kolkata—that would be home to many British transplants. The Company exported silk, sugar, tea, and opium out of India and imported English goods such as wool, silver, and other metals to India, growing wealthier and more powerful with each passing year.

The dominant ruling power in India at the time the East India Company showed up was the Mughal Empire, descendants of the Mongol Empire who were living in Turkestan in the fifteenth century. They had become Muslims and assimilated the culture of the Middle East, while also keeping elements of their Far Eastern roots. They were known for their great military skill and intolerance of Hindus.

Aurangzeb was the last great Mughal Emperor. He ruled for fifty years and to borrow a phrase from Dickens, it was the best of times, but it would also prove to be the worst of times. Aurangzeb ascended to the throne after having his father imprisoned and his older brother killed. His military ambition resulted in the expansion of the Mughal Empire to its greatest size ever. He was a devout Muslim who was unwilling to allow members of other faiths to openly practice their beliefs by ending the policy of religious tolerance that the previous emperors had followed. Hindus were no longer allowed to live under their own laws and customs; they had to abide by Islamic, or Sharia, law. Thousands of Hindu temples and shrines were torn down, and a punitive tax on Hindu subjects was imposed. Aurangzeb also invaded and conquered Hindu kingdoms in central and southern India, putting many of the residents into slavery.

While the Mughal Empire reached the peak of its military power under Aurangzeb, India's stability was crumbling, both because of his extreme social and cultural policies but also because the country had become too big to be effectively governed by his administration.

A Muslim governor in southern India rebelled, establishing a separate Shi'a state and instating religious tolerance. The Hindu kingdoms also rebelled, often supported by either the French or the British, which used the conflicts to increase their country's footprint on the subcontinent. A turning point in India's history came when the East India Company took control of Calcutta in 1696.

In the early 1700s, with the Mughal Empire imploding, other countries saw a possible opportunity to claim their own stakes. The biggest threat to the Company was France, which began seizing British trading posts. The East India Company started hiring its own armies to defend the trading posts. The conflict with the French came to a head at the Battle of Plassey in 1757.

Shirajuddula, the governor of Bengal, had a large, skilled army and significant ammunitions. However, his commander, Mirjafar, betrayed Shirajuddula to advance his own political ambitions. He made a pact with the British that he would not send his troops when the British army were attacking, so despite being vastly outnumbered, the East India Company's forces defeated Indian forces backed by the French. After Shirajuddula was defeated and executed—and after paying a large sum of money to the British—Mirjafar's goal to become governor of Bengal came to fruition. Eight years later after Mirjafar's death, the Company subsequently took possession of Bengal, an important region of northeastern India, which greatly increased its holdings.

Considering the power it ultimately wielded, it's easy to forget the East India Company started simply as a private trade venture. But the decline of the Mughal Empire that had coincided with the rise of regional powers gave the Company an opportunity to entrench itself in India's affairs. And what began as a commercial enterprise gradually became a military and diplomatic organization with tremendous power and influence that came to literally rule India. The East India Company was grabbing land, taxing, and torturing people with the support of the British government. They were also involved in converting Hindus, the predominant population in India, to Christianity against protests. These practices by the company led to unrest and increasing tensions within the Indian people. But even as the

Company's political domination increased, its trading interests—meaning, profits—were never lost sight of. But just as with Aurangzeb, overreaching expansion and greed would prove the Company's undoing.

In the late 1700s East India executives became infamous for returning to London where they would flaunt their enormous wealth. These officials became known as *nabobs*. Although derived from the Mughal word for a leader, it was a sarcastic term that came to connote an idle, profligate, or extravagant lifestyle. As often is the case, where there is great power and wealth, there is also great corruption. Disturbed by reports of rampant corruption taking place essentially unchecked in India, the British government decided to step in and assert some control over the East India Company's affairs by appointing a man named Warren Hastings as the first governor-general to oversee it. That didn't go as planned either. Hastings was impeached when members of Parliament grew resentful at the nabobs' continually growing wealth.

The next governor-general of the Company was Lord Cornwallis, who was known in both Britain and the newly formed United States as the British officer who had surrendered to General George Washington in the Battle of Yorktown in Virginia, essentially ending the American Revolution. Cornwallis served as governor-general until 1793, and during his tenure he did institute reforms that helped root out the corruption that enabled Company employees to amass huge personal fortunes.

Richard Wellesley, who served as governor-general in India from 1798 to 1805, was pivotal in expanding the Company's power by ordering the invasion of Mysore, which began decades of military conquests and territorial acquisitions for the East India Company. So much so that in 1833 the British Parliament passed the Government of India Act that ended the Company's trading business, making it the de facto government in India.

In 1844, English was declared the official language. Also beginning in the 1840s, governor-general Lord Dalhousie implemented a policy called Doctrine of Lapse to acquire even more territory by declaring that if an Indian ruler died without an heir, or was known to be incompetent, the British could take their territory. It should be noted that while the Company—and by extension Britain—was controlling a lot of territory, there was a lot they didn't. There were hundreds of independent principalities throughout the subcontinent that controlled their claimed areas. But by using this doctrine, the Company expanded their territory and increased their income. However, it was quickly recognized that the blatant land grab was increasing tensions with the Indian people. There were also religious issues. The East India Company had allowed Christian missionaries to spread their religion's word, convincing Indians that the British were intent on converting the subcontinent to Christianity.

The rumors didn't stop there. In the late 1850s a new rifle bullet was introduced, where the cartridge was wrapped in grease-coated paper. The idea was the grease made it easier for the bullet to move through the rifle barrel. But a false rumor started among the native soldiers the Company employed, called *sepoys*, that the grease used on the paper was derived from cows and pigs. According to the Islamic dietary law, pork is considered unclean, and eating it is forbidden. Similarly, Hindus are forbidden to eat most animal-based foods, such as beef. So, this rumor had both Muslim and Hindu sepoys believing the British were trying to undermine India's religions. (Just shows you how political-based misinformation isn't unique to our modern times.) But the Company did not pay enough attention to the growing level of discontent about this and other policies that led Indians to believe Britain was trying to eliminate their traditional culture. The result was the Indian Revolt of 1857, a brief but bloody conflict against the rule of the East India Company that resulted in the loss of many lives.

In response to the uprising, the British Parliament passed the Government of India Act of 1858, which ended the company's role in India and declared that India would be governed by the British crown, thus beginning India's colonial era. The government also dissolved the Company, and three years later its opulent headquarters in London, East India House, was torn down. But the exploitation, physical torture, execution, and undue arrests of the people continued, which led to a rising tide of nationalism.

While there is no argument from our current perspective that British rule was often racist and exploitive, it also laid the foundation for eventual Indian democracy and nationhood. Like a lot of relationships, it was complicated. In Paul Scott's novel, *The Jewel in the Crown*, he writes that India and Britain were "locked in an imperial embrace of such long-standing and subtlety it was no longer possible for them to know whether they hated or loved one another, or what it was that held them together."

There are two histories of India. The first is what the Western history books tell us. That India would be under British colonial rule from 1857 until 1947. During that time the people of India experienced many changes, some good, some not so much. Again, Britain only controlled about 60 percent of the subcontinent. However, learning from the East India Company's mistakes, the British established treaties with the various independent principalities instead of trying to conquer them with military force.

Traditionally, higher education was confined primarily to upper castes, but the British made education more accessible to all Indians. And it turned out that making English the official language meant that Indians from diverse regions who would traditionally speak different languages were now able to easily communicate through English. That newfound connection helped instill a sense of nationalism, especially among students.

The British also provided more job opportunities, from joining the military or going into civil service to working as day laborers, drivers, and servants for British expats. The British improved infrastructure, building roads, hospitals, schools, and other structures, including a railway system. These improvements were aimed at helping the British rule India and to resolve difficulties that indirectly helped the locals. Britain militarily protected India against potential invaders from Afghanistan, Persia, and other Western countries.

For those wealthy enough, the British allowed Indians to go to school and college in Britain. Among those who took that opportunity was Mahatma Gandhi. Being exposed to Western education and great thinkers like John Locke and Voltaire, gave Indian students inspiring ideas about freedom, equality, and democracy. Those ideas gradually swelled into a desire for change, a need for independence.

That rising tide of nationalism made running the empire increasingly challenging politically and economically. Britain was affected by US foreign policy that called for an end of Western imperialism. It seemed only a matter of time before India gained self-rule.

Then there is the history of those who lived it, whose perspective comes from the inside out. For example, the British made English the national language for better communication between the English and the Indians, and also between the Indians themselves as they spoke different languages in different parts of India. Another reason for it was to employ the English-speaking locals at a much lower salary than their English counterparts.

The English language exposed the students and the intellectuals to the Western culture, philosophy, literature, deductive logic, fairness, individual rights, and political freedom. Contemporary upheaval in Europe, Japan, Russia, and South America brought a new perspective to the newly English-educated Indian generation.

East India Company, under the military protection of the British Government, raised havoc in India. The company imported goods from overseas and sold them in India at a very high profit, then purchased Indian silk, tea, gold, and spices at a negligible price. They forced farmers to plant indigo and bought it at no price at all. The indigo plantations lasted for more than one hundred years and bankrupted wealthy landowners.

The deterioration of Indian arts, industries, and the steady impoverishment of the millions of Indians continued to bleed subcontinent resources to benefit Britain. The Empire progressed and prospered in every respect, but India became malnourished, and the British economy played a significant role in the history of Indian nationalism, a sociopolitical environment that produced many reformers, intellectuals, politicians, and writers.

Raja Rammohan Roy, probably the first reformer, created the Brahmo Society, a theistic movement within Hinduism, to expose the centuries-old superstition of Hindu religion, to prevent conversion to Christianity, and advocated for women's rights and education in the early nineteenth century. Another stalwart, Vidyasagar, with the help of the British legislature passed laws—in the face of severe criticism—to prevent wives being burned alive in the funeral pyres with their dead husbands, to ban polygamy, and to allow widows to remarry.

This era produced Bankim Chatterjee, a novelist and the prophet of Indian Nationalism, who coined the slogan *Bande Mataram* (Hail to the Motherland) in one of his patriotic novels, a term that reverberated throughout India during our freedom struggle and still does today.

Swami Vivekananda, a religious philosopher and a nationalist, gave his famous lecture on the Hindu religion at the historic Parliament of Religions in Chicago in 1893, giving young India visibility to the international forum.

Poet Rabindra Nath Tagore, a Nobel Laureate in literature, was active in the freedom movement. Two different poems of Tagore became the national anthems of India and Bangladesh after their independence.

S. N. Banerjee, the father of Indian Nationalism, and W. C. Banerjee formed the Indian National Congress party in 1888 in Calcutta, which subsequently became the main political force for India's independence movement. Dada Bhai Nawroji presided over that meeting. Mahatma Gandhi became president of the party in 1920 and carried out many anti-British movements. Throughout the nineteenth and twentieth centuries, India continued to demand independence through political agitations and disobedience.

One of Gandhi's successors, Subhas Chandra Bose was party president for two terms. Subhas Bose was placed under house arrest in Calcutta but escaped. He eventually went to Japan where he convinced Emperor Hirohito to turn over to him Indian soldiers held in captivity by the Japanese military in Malaysia. He formed the *Azad Hind Fouz* (Indian National Army) with the released Indian soldiers, and their slogan was *Jai Hind* (Victory to India). His army reached the eastern part of India toward the end of World War II. Bose died in a plane crash and failed to accomplish his goal.

Throughout the nineteenth and twentieth centuries, the British created havoc in India and for Indians. They extracted money from the people by taxation, exploitation, and denying payments with devastating consequences. People protested physical torture, sometimes violently, creating upheaval in the peace-loving society. Khudiram Bose, a nineteen-year-old patriot, was hanged in Bengal. There were many other hangings throughout India as well. Hundreds of young teenagers and adults, mainly from Bengal, were sent to a jail in the Andaman Islands and never returned.

I recently visited the Andaman jail and to my horror saw nooses hanging, five in a row, to hang the prisoners, their bodies to drop in a hole below. These prisoners were kept isolated in a very small cell, on a cement floor for a bed. The windows of the buildings were arranged in such a way that the prisoners could not see each other.

The British passed a law in 1919 that allowed the government to arrest anybody and keep them in jail without a trial. People protested all over India. On the morning of April 13th that year, thousands of people gathered at

Jallianwalla Bagh garden in the Punjab city of Amritsar to peacefully protest the arrest and deportation of two national leaders, Satya Pal and Saifuddin Kitchlew, and to honor the Sikh festival of Baisakhi.

Under the command of Acting Brigadier-General Reginald Dyer, troops of the British Indian Army fired rifles into the crowd of unarmed Indian civilians. The Jallianwalla Bagh public garden was walled on all sides. General Dyer blocked the main exits, and the troops continued firing until their ammunition ran out. More than a thousand people died. The press was barred from reporting the massacre for a month. Gandhi and other leaders had a muted response. Tagore was outraged, *renounced his knighthood* in protest and wrote a song:

My voice is throttled today. The flute has lost its voice.

The night is moonless. My world is lost under a nightmare.

Many other people were also gunned down as they protested all over India. Seventy-two-year-old revolutionary Matangini Hazra was shot and killed while leading a peaceful protest march of about five thousand women in Bengal.

It became challenging both politically and economically for Britain to run the Empire, and the calls for independence increased. World War II moved that process along. Mishandling of the massive Bengal Famine of 1943 caused an uproar internationally, and the associated Quit India movement became a crucial factor for independence. Britain's Labor Party, which always supported self-rule for India, came to power in 1945. At the same time, the United States was pressuring for the end of Western imperialism.

But the momentum to give India independence was complicated by the demand to create Pakistan as a separate and independent Muslim nation. Mohammed Ali Jinnah, leader of the Muslim League political party, called for the partition of India along religious lines in the Muslim-majority provinces of Punjab and Bengal. Eventually the British government and the Congress Party accepted partition.

After the war Britain had to make a practical decision. After so many years of war, there weren't the resources available to keep control of its jewel in the crown, so the government—along with the Indian National Congress—approved partition and embarked on a relatively rushed exit from India.

Viceroy Lord Mountbatten transferred power on August 15, 1947, and India became an independent nation. In hindsight the hasty retreat did not consider the potential consequences from such a swift transition of power—and some might argue carelessly drawn borders using out-of-date census material—that left the subcontinent partitioned into two independent nations: India with a Hindu majority was located between the newly formed country of East and West Pakistan. The Muslim dominated part of the state of Bengal became East Pakistan (now the country of Bangladesh), and the Hindu dominated part of Bengal became West Bengal and remained part of India. This would open the flood gates to extreme communal violence in Punjab and Bengal.

The new partitioning also prompted one of the largest human migrations in history—an estimated ten million—as Muslims headed to West and East Pakistan and Hindus and Sikhs tried to reach India. A combined million died trying.

Throughout the subcontinent, communities that had coexisted for nearly a thousand years started attacking one another in a mob-driven orgy of violence—mostly religion-driven—with Hindus and Sikhs in one corner and Muslims in the other. In the Punjab and Bengal states, which were located along India's borders with West and East Pakistan respectively, it was a human slaughterhouse. Massacres, arson, forced religious conversions, mass kidnapping, and disappearances were widespread. It is estimated seventy-five thousand women were raped. Afterward many were then disfigured or dismembered.

I remember an incident from around that time. The Hindu refugees who came from East Pakistan after losing everything, including family members who were killed, were infuriated. They tried to occupy the houses deserted by the local Muslims and were eager for revenge killing. It was early in the night, and we could hear the mob fury coming from a distance. There was a knock on the door. It was a Muslim couple, shaking in fear, as they ran away from the mob. My family took them in and assured them protection.

Somehow the mob found out that we were hiding the couple and demanded that we produce them or else they would kill us. My brothers called their bluff and invited them in to look for them—the couple was hiding in the cow-shed—however, the mob left. The next morning we brought them to the nearby nawab's house, which was converted into a protection camp.

The assassination of Mahatma Gandhi on January 30, 1948, by a Hindu fundamentalist enabled secularists within the government to assert more influence, leading to the ratification of a constitution and the first democratic elections in 1951, which made India the world's largest democracy.

In his book *The Post-American World,* Indian-American journalist Fareed Zakaria wrote:

India's democracy is truly extraordinary.... India's political system owes much to the institutions put in place by the British over two hundred years ago. In many other parts of Asia and in Africa, the British were a relatively temporary presence. They were in India for centuries. They saw it as the jewel in their imperial crown and built lasting institutions of government throughout the country—courts, universities, administrative agencies. But perhaps even more importantly, India got very lucky with the vehicle of its independence, the Congress Party, and its first generations of post-independence leaders, who nurtured the best traditions of the British and drew on older Indian customs to reinforce them.

Even though Congress was in charge, they invited opposition parties, women's rights groups, minorities, lower castes, atheists, secularists, socialists, defenders of landlords, and the general public to participate.

Pandit Jawaharlal Nehru was the Congress leader and the first Prime Minster of India. In a speech, "Objective Resolution," to the Constituent Assembly meeting in December of 1946, Nehru proposed India as an independent sovereign country, guaranteeing its citizens justice, equal opportunity, freedom of expression, and belief. The constitution also advocated rights to the minorities through progressive social change and national unity.

Many western writers and politicians proclaimed that an independent India would never survive. Winston Churchill was the staunchest critic against the independence of India, having once said "to abandon India to the rule of the Brahmans would be an act of cruel and wicked negligence." He predicted that the public services created by the British would be destroyed and felt India would "fall back quite rapidly through the centuries into the barbarism and privations of the Middle Ages."[1]

Contrary to that vision, India held its first election in 1951 and continues to do so to this day. India stands firm in its democratic principles after seven decades.

My generation straddled colonial India and independent India. The British left India even before I graduated from the high school. And as a result, we were much less influenced by the British system than the previous generation. I must say we benefitted from the establishment of the educational system, one of them being medicine. Of course, whether you were able to parlay that education into a successful career depended on just how hard you were willing to work. And I was very motivated.

---

[1] The above quotes are taken from *India after Gandhi: The History of the World's Largest Democracy* by Ramchandra Guha.

Kites, Cobras, and Cannabis

My hometown was bounded by two rivers which flowed through. The Karala, often referred to as the Thames of Jalpaiguri, snakes through the town, which is also located on the banks of the Teesta, the second largest river in West Bengal after the Ganges. The currents of the Teesta River could be ferocious during the monsoon season. The violent churning of the convulsing, foaming, roaring water made it difficult to hear each other standing on the shore. But in the winter, the river would be dry, and silky, velvety, soft sand would fill the riverbed. Alongside the river there were open fields studded with mango, coconut, grapefruit, jackfruit, and palm trees. All the schools were called *high school* and went from class three to ten, not grades. Children started high school when they were about eight—we were home schooled until then—and finished when they were in their teens. My school, Fanindra Deb Institution, popularly called FDI, was situated close to both rivers, making for a scenic vista.

Monday through Thursday we were given a daily half-hour recess; on Fridays it was an hour. My friends and I would spend the time playing soccer using the grapefruits we picked from nearby trees. We would always play barefoot. A lot of sports were played shoes-optional—even with leagues. The Indian field hockey team played barefoot in the Olympics, where they won six successive gold medals from 1928 to 1956.

But at my school we did not have organized athletics overseen by coaches or teachers. While each school in town had soccer and cricket teams that competed against each other, it was more or less organized by the students. But teachers did organize track and field events in the winter, with all the schools competing. That was a very colorful, exciting event. Prizes were given, food was provided, and all the townspeople came to cheer on the participants. But while enjoyed, sports were not a main focus; education was. At home, parents maintained strict discipline about studying and doing well in school because they wanted us to achieve more than they had.

But taking school seriously didn't mean not having fun or being kids. During the recess a group of us would occasionally go pick some mangoes, skin it with the knives some of us carried, then eat them even though these pitiful mangoes were so sour they made our teeth pucker. But the bigger attraction was a local orchard, crowded with many grapefruit, mango, coconut, and betel nut trees. The orchard, which was fenced in precisely to keep interlopers like my friends and me out, belonged to a wealthy man who lived there with his daughters and sons. Now and then when the security guards were either not looking—or not caring and ignored us— we would sneak into the orchard to pick some grapefruits to play soccer with and betel nuts to chew. Betel nuts are very popular in India and chewed with betel leaves, which is known as pan.

One day after playing soccer in the fields, we went to the orchard to collect some betel nuts. As usual we were barefoot. It had rained a little that particular Friday, which made the ground and trees slippery. One of the boys in our group, Badol, was an expert climber. Betel nut trees—or more accurately, areca palm trees—were fifty or sixty feet tall and the nuts were found in bunches on the top fronds. The plan was for Badol to climb up, pick the nuts, and then drop them down where ground boys would gather them and run to the fence where the rest of us outside the fence would collect them.

We did several runs before the security guards showed up. The guys waiting for the dropped nuts fled and jumped over the fence. The trouble was, Badol was on the top of the tree, and the security guards were standing at the bottom, so he could not come down without getting apprehended. We somehow managed to distract the guards, and Badol scurried down the tree trunk, sprinted to the fence, and vaulted over it. The security guards, bamboo batons in hand, ran after him but slipped and fell on the wet grass.

We were safe!

To get back to the school, we had to walk through a cemetery and the orchard from the playground. On our way we heard the school bell ring, heralding the start of the class. Knowing that we would be late and not wanting to get in trouble, we decided to hide under the windows then climb into the classroom at the end of the class. Windows were always open, and they were not very high from the ground. At the end of the class when the bell rang again, we quickly climbed through the windows into the classroom and sat in our respective seats.

The room had wooden benches that sat five students at a long desk that held schoolbooks. If the books were on the desk with no student behind them, the teacher would know who was absent. Students did not move from class to class; the teachers did. The new teacher coming into the room to start the next class would not be aware we hadn't been in the previous class. The instruction started, and we felt safe but not for long. Somebody had informed the headmaster, Kalinga Babu, about our absence, and we were summoned to his office.

Now we were scared; not only because of the potential punishment but because our parents would be notified. As we approached the office, the headmaster's assistant told us to wait outside. The owner of the orchard was talking to our headmaster. He had complained before about kids, but this time it was special.

We panicked.

After the owner left, the headmaster called us in, sharply scolded us, told us not to do it again, then sent us back to the class. We had dodged the proverbial bullet. At the time we felt that he was a great headmaster; I still do all these years later. We were ten- to twelve-year-old boys getting into benign mischief, and the verbal punishment he doled out did fit the "crime."

All in all, the school days in Jalpaiguri were very pleasant, congenial, and satisfying. In addition to studying, we were involved in many extra-curricular activities. I loved to play soccer, cricket, and kite flying. I played soccer all over Jalpaiguri for my school, for my team, and was hired by other teams. There were some remarkable events that happened which come to my mind as I reminisce.

We used to fly kites in the winter months after our final examination of the class was over. I would spend all day flying kites with my brothers Kalu and Dilu. The main thing that we needed was a *latai*, a cylindrical reel or spindle with handles that held the thread attached to the kite. The priciest store-bought ones looked like works of art, made of nice wood or bamboo, with attractive shapes, colors, length, and dimensions. They varied in size from six inches to two feet long.

Some kite flyers were expert spinners; we were ragtag kite flyers and made our own latai. We'd take a spool of thread and slide it onto a stick so it could easily spin. Then one person would hold the spool stick and the other would attach the end of the thread to a cylindrical can, bamboo sticks bound together, or any type of round discs, be they metal, wood, or even cardboard. Then by spinning the latai handles in your fingers, you'd transfer the thread from the spool to the latai. As long as we could spin it, we were happy.

The thread around the cylinder had to be made sharp by applying finely mashed glass on the thread. First, we'd collect shards of broken glass and use a mortar and pestle to grind them into a fine powder. That glass would be mixed with glue made of mashed cooked rice or a flour dough. We would then stake two five- or six-foot bamboo poles into the ground a few feet apart and tie the free end of the thread to one of the poles. One of us would take the latai and walk between the poles, unrolling the thread around the poles; the other would follow and apply the glass mix to the thread. Then we'd let it dry before rolling the thread back onto the latai. In all it would take several hours to complete the process. Then you just hoped the thread was of good quality to withstand a kite fight.

In the process of mixing the glass dough and applying it to the threads, there was always a possibility of lacerating your finger. When it happened we'd gather some marigold leaves, squish it with a little water, and press it against the cut. There was no running to the ER, no sutures, and no tetanus shots. We did just fine, but I do not recommend that now.

The kite itself was made of thin, different colored paper, like wrapping paper, and was diamond shaped. We'd glue a straight thin bamboo stick along the center of the kite and another thin bendable bamboo stick in the shape of a rainbow would be placed along the edges. They were tied together with thread where they intersected, leaving a short tail of the thread. Another tie would be placed in the center of the kite around the bamboo stick, again with a short tail left. These two tails of the thread would be tied together in a triangle, and the free end of the main thread would be tied to that triangle, which controlled maneuvering the kite.

Then it was time to fly the kite. One of us would walk with the kite for about twenty to thirty feet, and wait for a small gust of wind, then we threw the kite towards the sky. You'd gain some height by manipulating the thread. When the kite reached twenty to thirty feet high, it would catch the wind and keep soaring. Depending on the length of the latai thread, it would go so high that it would twinkle like a little star.

I could make the kite fly left or right for a long distance with great speed, make the kite dive in a wide or a narrow circle, dive it down almost to the ground, and bring it right up to its height. Sometimes, I would stake one end of the handle in the ground, make the kite spin and spin around the thread way up in the sky. You just sit, relax, chit chat with your brother or friend, and watch the kite spin. It was so wonderful, and it's difficult to express in words the pleasure we derived from it.

But I had to keep alert because if suddenly another kite came flying next to mine, that meant a kite fight—which was exactly what we wanted. It was so thrilling. To win the fight the kite had to go around in a circle in a tight loop around the other kite's thread making a knot, then a sharp pull up in the sky would cut the thread and the other kite floated away in defeat. To not let the other guy go over my thread, I would fly parallel to the kite. If the other kite was diving down, I would dive down; if he was going up, I would go up or go left or right and deny him the upper hand. We might stop the fight and go our own way. Most of the time we wouldn't be able to see the person flying the other kite. He might be in the next neighborhood. All you'd see were the kites. These battles were so exhilarating, so exciting, that I would do it all day, sometimes forgetting to eat lunch.

That love of kite flying never left me. Years later I was on a Martha's Vineyard beach to try my hand again even though it had been many years since I'd last flown a kite. I had brought some kites and a latai back from a recent trip to India. American kites are larger, heavier, have tails, and the thicker thread is pulled with bare hands; there's no latai. But they can also withstand a lot of wind, which was very strong on the beach. I wasn't sure my fine thread and thin, small kite could withstand the gusts blowing off the ocean.

But my kite was not intimidated by the wind. I got it in the air and performed up, down, right, and left movements. I also tried small circles and when that worked I decided to try diving the kite down almost to the sand then pull it up. While I was doing that, I heard a couple walking by comment that the kite was going to hit the ground. To their surprise I pulled it up and felt that old familiar thrill and could have stayed on the beach for hours. I have not flown a kite again since that day, but the memories will always be with me. In some ways I think it's literally in our blood.

The tradition of kite flying in India is ancient and is believed to have been brought into the country by Chinese visitors. But Chinese kites were rectangular and flat tools used for measuring distances, signaling, and also for communicating military operations. Indian kites can look like works of art. In certain parts of India, they are now used as an expression of patriotism and freedom on our Independence Day, which is August 15th, but where I grew up, we just use kites for sport and enjoyment.

Another popular pastime was going to the movies. We had half-day school on Fridays. As soon as class was let out, we would run to the lone movie house showing Tarzan movies. Tickets were sold about fifteen minutes before the start through a cubby hole dominated by the local bullies. Everybody would make a big fracas as soon as the window opened.

There was no way that straggling kids like us would get into the lines to buy a ticket. We had to know big guys to buy our tickets for us. It did not matter how many tickets we bought because we had a system for everybody to get in. We had to sit on wooden benches in front of the screen. We would wait in nervous anticipation for Tarzan to swing from a tree branch to rescue Jane from either a tiger, people, or floodwater. The hall would erupt in ear-splitting applause after the rescue. It was a fashion for us to pose like the muscle man Johnny Weissmuller.

Festivals were also a big part of our social lives. *Holi* or *Dol* is an annual festival of color celebrated all over India on the day of the full moon, *Dol Purnima*, in March. *Purnima* means *full moon* in Sanskrit. In some parts of India, on the eve of Holi, large bonfires are lit to mark the occasion and to burn evil spirits. In the states of West Bengal and Odisha, the Holi festival is celebrated as *Dol Jatra*, which is dedicated to Krishna. One of the traditions of the festival is to smear people's faces with red-colored powder, usually made from herbs, called *abir*. Colored water is also sprayed with a squirt gun covering the whole body. We would carry the powder in our shirt pockets or in packets then walk around in the streets or go to friend's and neighbor's houses and smear each other with abir. It was full of fun and frolic and as kids we always looked forward to it.

On one Dol day when I was probably ten or twelve years old, Kalu and I went celebrating with our pockets filled with abir. We were having great fun smearing our friends—and getting smeared. We went to Raja's house, one of Kalu's friends, and were smearing each other with gusto. But as I rubbed abir on Raja's face, I suddenly could not breathe. I was having stridor—an abnormal, high-pitched breathing sound caused by a blockage in the throat or larynx—and soon could not see. My face, tongue, and throat were all burning. I sustained burns on my face, mouth, and my eyes.

There was a big commotion, and Raja's father came out of the house. They immediately took me to the hospital where doctors treated me and sent me home. For two weeks after, I still could not see and could only drink liquids with difficulty. My family would guide me to the living room, and I would sit there talking to my friends, wishing I could go outside with them. Up until then, I didn't realize I had so many friends. I was just hoping I'd be able to see them again.

My father used to take me to the hospital for my appointments in a rickshaw. Raja's father offered their car, but my father declined as a matter of pride. At each visit doctors would clean my eyes and do other treatments. Fortunately, the breathing problem resolved quickly, and my eyes gradually recovered, thanks to the doctors at the hospital. The experience made me that much more appreciative of the power of healing.

As far as my mystery ailment, Raja eventually admitted he'd had a small bottle of ammonia in his shirt pocket. The pressure of the ammonia's vapors pushed the cork out like a champagne bottle, spraying my face with the caustic chemical when I was smearing abir on him.

That was definitely not the spirit of Dol.

Outdoors was filled with all manner of flora and fauna. When I was about five or six years old, I took a walk with my older sister, Kaku. On both sides of the road were wide open fields filled with wildflowers. During the monsoon season these fields would be inundated with water, and hyacinths, lotuses, and other indigenous plants would bloom. At night, the croaking of frogs would fill the darkness.

At the end of the road was an empty plot of land, probably for building a home. A brick wall that rose from the street level surrounded the plot as a foundation. A part of the wall had broken and the bricks were strewn on the ground. I jumped from the plot, which was a few feet high, to the brick wall. On landing I felt something soft squirming under my feet—as usual, I was barefoot. When I jumped the second time, I felt the velvety squirming again.

I told my sister and we both looked among the fallen bricks and found a golden-brown baby snake coiled up in the empty space. Fortunately, it was a non-poisonous variety. We often came upon small snakes. Occasionally, we would grab the snake by the tail, twirl it around. and throw it away—which I cannot even think of doing now. This time the small snake quickly slithered away, and so did we.

One day I came home from school and walked into pandemonium. Most of my family—and many of our neighbors—were standing outside our house. They breathlessly explained there was a large snake inside our house, presumably a king cobra. My mother was inside frying a concoction of turmeric, red chili pepper, and whatever else. According to an old wives' tale, the pungent, irritating, eye-watering vapors would drive the snake away. It didn't. But it sure drove my siblings out of the house.

Snakes are a fact of life in India. More than 10 percent of the approximately two thousand species of snakes found in the world are found there, ranging from the four-inch worm snake to eighteen-foot pythons and king cobras. Fortunately, the vast majority of snakes that call India home are non-venomous, but that doesn't make them any more welcome.

The snake was hiding—somewhere—and did not come out. Some of us were looking for one of the snake charmers who used to come around, but we couldn't locate one.

A man walked up and asked what was happening. He introduced himself as a handyman and said he was on his way home from working in a field. He had a burlap sack with him and to our relief volunteered to catch the snake. He went inside our house and quickly located the snake coiled up and resting in a corner of our bathing area. The snake was probably just looking for a moist, cool area and our bathing area, which had a smooth cement floor, was open on one side, and walled on the other three sides with no roof, provided perfect reptile accommodations. The man managed to get the snake into the burlap sack and carried it away.

Everyone was relieved and happy, until my mother insisted we wash down the entire house. To get water from our well, we used a pulley system. We hooked the bucket to a bamboo pole that was weighted on the end by bricks. We had to make many trips that day to get enough water to clean the house to my mother's satisfaction.

And yes, snake charmers really existed; they were not just a fiction of Hollywood/Bollywood movies. When I was growing up snake charmers were a fixture at Indian markets and festivals, sitting cross-legged on the ground thrilling everyone with their ability to control cobras and sometimes other venomous snakes. You really believed the snake was listening to the charmer's flute-like instrument, which in my area was called a *banshi, (pronounced as baashi)*. The charmer seemed to hypnotize the snake into submission by gently swaying to the music. I later realized it was the Indian version of a carnival sideshow—more con than magic.

For one thing, snakes can't hear musical notes because they don't have ears. They navigate by picking up surrounding vibrations. What looks like hypnosis is merely intense focus on the bansi, which the snake perceives as a potential threat. The snake sways along with the charmer to keep its focus on the instrument.

The majority of charmers respected their cobras because they are part of our culture. The Hindu god Shiva is usually portrayed wearing a king cobra around his neck, and there is even an annual festival, Nag Panchami, that honors the king cobra. But unfortunately, a small number of charmers would abuse the snakes by breaking off their fangs so they couldn't bite even if they wanted to. The most unscrupulous would even sew the creature's mouth shut. Not only couldn't it bite, it also couldn't eat, and the snake would eventually starve to death.

These abuses led to a 1972 law that forbids anyone in India to keep a snake, although for decades it was rarely enforced. But in recent years as snake populations have become threatened, the government is trying to balance culture with wildlife management by allowing snake charmers to keep any existing snake, while preventing the capture of any more. Perhaps it is inevitable the snake charmers of old will go the way of blacksmiths and the art will disappear. But like the man with the burlap bag who removed the snake from our house, some environmentalists are trying to use snake charmers as snake rescuers. Instead of performing at festivals and exploiting the animals, the charmers are being hired to remove venomous snakes from city and suburban gardens and return them to the wild. While that may not be as magical as charming the cobra, or as haunting as the bansi melody, it seems like a good way to bridge the past with the present.

Another fact of life in the India I grew up in was growing your own vegetables. There was a small plot in front of our house that was used as a garden during the winter and spring. One of the vegetables, a kind of spinach, was called *sak*. It could be served cream style or steamed—however prepared, it was delicious. My mother also liked to experiment and cook sak mixed with other leafy vegetables such as *palong sak, lal sak*, and many others.

Our school day started late in the morning and ended in the afternoon. We would eat what essentially was brunch before going to school then have some rice and curry when we got home from school before going outside to play soccer or whatever mischief we'd get into. Like kids everywhere, we were to return home before it got dark. By then everybody would be up after their naps, the kerosene lamps would be lit, and we would have some food. Naps were part of the culture. The heat and humidity in India wear you down so a nap, a siesta, is a way to rejuvenate.

One day after returning from school, I ate a nice snack then went off to play soccer. When I returned home, the house was completely dark; no lamps were lit and everybody was still asleep. That was odd. Even odder was I had a difficult time waking everybody up. Nobody could understand why they all had slept so long and so deeply. I didn't think much of it. It was examination time at school, so I sequestered myself in a small room of the house, shutting the door and closing the window to prevent any distractions. But before long I became so tired, I could not stay awake.

When it was time for dinner, my mother sent one of my siblings to get me, but I didn't answer the door, which was locked. No matter how hard they pounded on the door, I didn't wake up. My family was now worried that something had happened to me. Maybe I had fallen and hit my head or been bitten by a snake that had snuck into our house—again.

They went outside and tried to open the window, but that was also locked, so they had one of my siblings run to get a carpenter, who came and opened the locked door just as my brother had somehow jimmied open the window and was poking me with a bamboo stick to wake me up. When I roused, I was surprised and confused to see so many people surrounding me. After they checked me over, I assured them I was fine; I just hadn't been able to keep my eyes open. It was strange that the entire family had suddenly become narcoleptic. By the next day the mysterious exhaustion had passed, but the puzzle of its cause remained unsolved.

A few days later my siblings and I were hanging out and talking in a room that overlooked the garden, which was separated from the road by a three-foot high wall that was lined with many tall plants. We were all shocked to see several guys jump on the wall, pull up those plants, and run away. Before we could even yell at them to stop, they were long gone. In trying to figure out what had just happened, it finally occurred to us why anyone would steal wild plants—it must be cannabis, which we called ganza plants. My family not only didn't indulge in ganza, they did not even recognize the plant.

Then the light bulb went off over our collective heads. We asked our mother about the plants that had been growing along the wall, and she acknowledged that a few days ago—the day nobody could stay awake—she had harvested leaves from the plants and mixed them with the sak. Mystery solved. And since the thieves had taken all the plants, we didn't have to worry about our mother inadvertently drugging us again.

When I was in ninth or tenth grade, I went with a friend to the Jalpaiguri Medical School's annual open house. There were many jars containing anatomical specimens and medical student volunteers making demonstrations. There were also many corpses—not something you would see at an American medical school's open house. But as a kid I didn't consider it odd; it was fascinating, so I observed the specimens and corpses with deep interest and unabashed curiosity. The annual event concluded with a musical performance; I was in heaven. I loved watching musical shows and completely lost track of time. When it ended, my friend and I realized it was late, close to midnight, and hurriedly left.

It was about a twenty-minute walk home, and we were both somewhat scared because of being out in the dead of night and for what was awaiting us at home. It was a cool night with moonlight illuminating the streets. At that hour the town was eerily quiet, the streets deserted. My house was down a narrow, gravel road off the main drag. The moonlight and tree branches created fearful shadows that had my imagination in overdrive. As I hurried toward my house, I heard footsteps in the distance and saw a kerosene lamp moving in the dark but whoever—or whatever—was carrying it remained invisible. I looked to my right toward a potato field and saw a woman in a white sari standing in one corner looking like a ghost. I was so frightened that I ran back to the main street.

Between the cadavers I'd seen earlier, the lamp floating on its own, and the specter of a woman, my juvenile senses were overloaded. After taking a moment to collect my wits, I knew I had to go home—ghost or no ghost. I ran as fast as I could down the gravel road toward my house, keeping my eyes focused straight ahead.

When I woke up the next morning, in the light of day the terrors of the previous night seemed far away, so I made my way back to the potato field, where I found a scarecrow dressed in white propped up with some bamboo sticks. And the lantern had been lighting the way for someone out walking. So even though the medical school's open house corpses and other exhibits might have turbo-charged my imagination and monsters-under-the-bed fears, it had still made me want to pursue medicine more than ever.

Land of Famine

We had a large family—I was one of thirteen children—and everybody lived together under one roof, even the adult siblings. Our financial situation was not always good. My father was an honest, straightforward, and principled man. Before moving to Jalpaiguri in the state of Bengal during the 1940s, he had worked as a government employee making a modest wage. His boss was English, and the other employees used to do the man's house chores. It was obviously outside of their official job description, but they were too afraid of getting fired to refuse. My father, though, did refuse and was transferred to a very wretched place where he lived in a waterlogged, snake-infested house. They also froze his pay increases, which in essence limited the amount his future pension would be because your pension would increase with each salary increase. He eventually retired from government work with a much smaller pension than he should have had.

I don't know if that experience fueled any nationalistic leanings, but for as long as I could remember, both my parents burned with patriotic fervor and protested against English rule, especially my mother. They joined the Swadeshi Movement—*swadeshi* means *of our own country*—which called for boycotting English and other foreign goods and only buying Indian-made products.

More impactful to everyone was the severe food shortage that Bengal suffered during World War II. Historians give various reasons for the famine—Japan's invasion of Burma, crop failure, redirecting resources to British troops—but regardless of the cause, more than three million people literally starved to death, many of them children, in the Bengal famine during 1943 and 1944.

It was the tradition of Indian society that the oldest son take over as head of the family household when the father retires. That was workable for the people with money; for low or middle-class families, not so much. My eldest brother, Dada, and our father purchased some farmland and a plot to build our house using my father's meager pension money. The farmland was very fertile and produced more rice than the neighboring lands because my brother had done his research, using good fertilizer and good seeds.

Even though I was only about seven years old, I still remember the sounds of the oxcarts arriving early in the cold winter morning fog. The farmers would unload the rice, vegetables, and fruits, and then we used to take hayrides on the ox cart. We also had cows, and I loved to watch calves being born. Cows were kept in a cowshed behind the house and gave birth in an open yard inside the house. We would sit for hours to watch the baby be born, then the cow would lick its newborn clean. Initially when the calf would try to stand up, it would fall. But in a matter of minutes, the calf would stand, jump, and run around. Amazing.

The milkman would come very early in the morning, milk the cows, and leave the milk on the verandah for later consumption. We had a bountiful supply of food when the famine started. The Bengal Famine of 1943 was a major disaster in British India during World War II. People called it a manmade Holocaust.

Bengal produced more than one-third of India's rice. But the development of railroads through cultivable lands for the military disrupted and severely damaged crop production. And a rapid population increase from soldiers coming to the area combined with decades of declining rice production, set the stage for a long-term fall in per capita availability of rice and an increase of landless laborers.

Outside availability was also getting closed off. India historically imported rice from Burma (now Myanmar). But in 1942 Burma fell to the Japanese, and the British banned importing rice from there, anticipating that the Japanese would invade India through Bengal. As a result, the cost of rice in Bengal became too expensive for most people to afford.

The fall of Burma brought hundreds of soldiers from Britain, the United States, China, and India to Calcutta and other parts of Bengal, resulting in local shortages of supplies, including rice. The military purchased farmlands, sometimes entire villages, to build airstrips and military camps. Millions of Bengalis were displaced.

The British military thought the Japanese would invade through the eastern part of Bengal. In 1942 the

British implemented the Denial of Rice and the Denial of Boat policies. They severely restricted the purchase of rice by local people and confiscated more than 40,000 boats, thereby denying the livelihood of the Bengali fishermen. The military also destroyed rice to deny the Japanese in case they came through. Food prices rose, and the first signs of famine started to appear in July 1942. The Bengal government started distributing rice and services to the workers in essential war industries by taking rice away from the starving rural districts.

Political parties, particularly in Calcutta, vehemently protested the astronomical price of rice. In 1942 the government fixed the price at such a low cost that rice disappeared into the black market. In May 1943 the first deaths from starvation in Bengal were reported. Churchill could have avoided the disastrous famine by sending food to Bengal, but his war cabinet refused to allow importing rice for Bengal despite repeated requests by the government.

Between May and October of 1943, people were dying of starvation. Families were abandoning or selling their children. Women were sexually abused or prostituted. Crying children lined up for miles outside the cities, particularly at night, for food. Children were seen picking through diarrheal discharge for undigested food grains they could eat. Most families that left their rural villages hoping to reach Calcutta for food died by the roadside, their skulls and bones visible for months after the famine.

Disposal of corpses was a massive problem. Corpses were stacked along the streets of Calcutta. The bodies were picked over by the vultures and dragged away by the jackals, sometimes when they were still alive. The living would drag bodies to open ditches.

The poorest in Bengal also suffered a cloth famine. India produced large amounts of textiles, and the military used most of it, exporting it to England. People started robbing graveyards for clothes, or literally took the clothes off of someone's back. Many women took turns sharing garments so they could venture out in public.

In 1944, the British started to bring food to Bengal and distributed it to the poorest residents. Bengal also had a bumper harvest. Gradually things were getting better, and starvation was reduced but not eliminated for a long time. The famine was another factor to hasten India's freedom, as it fueled the Quit India movement and spurred other protests.

Britain never officially declared a famine. If they had, the Famine Code could have been used for sizable aid. Media was not allowed to publish reports of famine. The political artist Chittaprosad Bhattacharya published five hundred pictures of "Hungry Bengal," and a thousand copies were destroyed. One surviving copy is in the Delhi Arts Museum.

Tony Blair apologized on Britain's behalf for the 1840s potato famine in Ireland, but no British prime minister has ever apologized for the Bengal famine.

Even though I was a little boy, I vaguely remember emaciated women with skeletonized babies on their hips coming to the door crying for food.

The mothers, in their weak, quivering voices, would cry out, "*Ma, ektu bhater jawl dow. Ektu bhat dow.*" ("Please give a little rice water. Please give a little rice.")

They were haunting. The house was kept dark and the barely clothed shapes of human bodies, particularly on a moonlit night, produced an eerie feeling.

Our harvest from the farmland tided us over the

famine, and we did not feel the hunger. But that was not to be for long. I heard that the jealous landowners around our farm wanted to grab our land because of our much better produce. A rumor was spread that the military was to lay down railroad tracks through the middle of our land and that selling the land would avoid a total loss. Dada was managing the farm but suffered from recurrent bouts of malaria and had to come home to recuperate. Inexperience and ill health pushed my brother and my father to sell the land at a very low price.

Dada went to Calcutta to look for a job after failing in local businesses but was unable to earn money quickly. In a joint family system, everybody pitches in. However, my other brothers were just about getting out of college with no jobs in sight. Years later my brother Kalu discovered a letter one of my other brothers had written to Dada in mid-1944 that said our mother had only one torn sari to wear and had stopped eating at night. Dada, being the eldest brother, was responsible to send some money home. At the time the younger children were kept totally in the dark regarding our dire situation, and it would take a long time to improve our financial footing.

Rising to the Challenges

As I said before, we did not like shoes. We walked, ran, and played all kinds of sports barefoot including soccer and cricket.

One day I was playing soccer in a rain-soaked field with glass shards strewn about. Unfortunately, I sustained a cut in my big toe and was bleeding rather a lot. I came home, and of course I sought my mother's help. My mother collected some marigold leaves from our garden. She washed the leaves in plain water, muddled it, and applied it to the cut and put a simple bandage of a cut piece of clean discarded sari. The bleeding stopped quickly, and the cut healed in no time.

I wanted to be a physician from my young age. I was fascinated by healing. My experience of facial trauma from the ammonia, my visit to the local medical school, observation of the anatomy specimens and the cadavers definitely, maybe indirectly, influenced my desire to go to medical school. When visiting the hospital, I was impressed by the surgeons in their scrubs as they talked to the families, and it inspired me to become a surgeon.

We had a ten-year curriculum in our schooling system at that time. At the end of ten years, we would take the final examination which was known as the Matriculation Examination. I graduated from the school when I was not quite fifteen.

Kalu was studying at Vidyasagar College in Calcutta and was satisfied. I enrolled there too but did not like it, so I went back to Jalpaiguri and joined the AC College for a two-year course. The curriculum was somewhat like today's STEM education that focuses on science, technology, engineering, and mathematics. It was geared toward going into undergraduate engineering, a pure science such as physics and chemistry, or medical school. Two years in college went by very quickly. We studied physics, chemistry, and biology. Biology was my favorite subject; I loved to dissect the frogs and examine the beating hearts.

At the end of two years, we had to take a theoretical and practical examination, which were given about two weeks apart. After finishing the theoretical examination, a group of us decided on a whim to go on a bicycle trip to go visit one of our friends in the tea gardens—one hundred miles away. Two of us started from our hometown,

Jalpaiguri. We left without any preparation or provisions, save for a hand pump to inflate the tires of our bikes, which were just ordinary single-speed, fixed-gear models, with small ringing bells for horns that would never get the attention of a car about to sideswipe you. We didn't worry about not having spare tires or a specific itinerary we could give our families; it was an adventure!

We left somewhat late in the day, and our first stop was about thirty miles away in Siliguri to pick up Sushanta, who was joining us. We had some tea at his house and worked out our route, which would take us through high mountains and forests and across some bridges and rivers. We had a hearty meal that night and a scrumptious breakfast the next morning before starting our journey.

The day was sunny, cool, and crisp. The roads were narrow with mountains on one side and steep cliffs on the other. The roads we rode on were the main thoroughfares for the trucks carrying goods. We couldn't let the picturesque surroundings distract us from carefully navigating the passing traffic.

We rode about forty miles a day, making frequent stops. Nobody carried bottled water back then so when thirsty we'd stop at a roadside tea stall to rest, hydrate with tea or water, and eat some snacks.

Our route took us across the Sevok Bridge, which spanned the Teesta River. During monsoon season the river was wild and treacherous. But we were there in the spring when it was calm and welcoming. The approach to the bridge was a steep downhill grade; past it was an equally steep incline. Our plan was to go down the steep approaching hill as fast as we could, believing the momentum would carry us up and over the incline on the other side.

As we neared the bridge, we could hear the murmur of the river. Soon the bridge appeared, the river flowing underneath. The water was crystal clear, its mild current creating ripples around small boulders. On the other side of the bridge, a pine-covered mountain touched the gorgeous clear blue sky. Flowers, including rhododendrons, junipers, roses, and marigolds added to the beauty of the scenery. The sun was hot, and the river looked so inviting, I wished we could dive in the cool water. However, we could not enjoy the scenery; we came down the hill at a high speed, flew across the bridge, and went up the mountain incline on the other side but only for a short distance; our momentum was no match for the incline.

The road curved around the mountain with a deep cliff on the other side that overlooked the river. At that point we had to walk our bikes because the road's incline was so steep. The road was so winding we felt the vibration of an oncoming truck before we could see it or even hear it honking. As soon as we felt the ground shake or heard the horn, we had to move to one edge of the road or the other until they passed. Small waterfalls coming down the mountain spilled onto the road, making them slick and slippery. But that was better than moving to the cliffside, which was frightening with its hundred-foot drop to the river.

Many years later I rode down that same steep road with my then-young sons, who were fervently saying Hail Marys the entire way down. Even in a car it seemed death-defying and thinking back I marveled at our youthful adventure using bicycles.

The sun was setting, and the day was coming to an end by the time we were able to get back on our bikes. Even though we wanted to go a little further, we were all tired.

Our bottoms were so painful from the hard bicycle seats we could hardly sit down. We reached a tea garden—what Americans might call a plantation or farm—and settled in their pleasant bungalow, where we were able to shower, change clothes, and have a good dinner.

The next morning, we ate breakfast then resumed our journey. After spending the entire day on the road, riding through picturesque mountains, forests, and tea gardens, we finally reached our friend Utpal's house, which was perched on a mountaintop with a 360-degree view and located in a tea garden his father managed. Their home was surrounded by waves of mountains covered with green tea plants, which are several feet high. When it came time to harvest the tea, female workers would pluck two leaves and a bud then place them in baskets they'd carry on their backs, supported by a band across their foreheads. But it was not yet the season for plucking so we would not see that. Instead we were treated to a dramatic torrential rainstorm with wind gusts up to about 40 or 50 miles per hour.

Such heavy rains arrive with the monsoon. Although many people in America think a monsoon is another term for the storm itself, the word actually refers to an annual seasonal shift in the wind. In the Indian Ocean and Southern Asia, the wind generally blows from the southwest during the spring and summer, roughly late April to the middle of October, and from the northeast during fall and winter, from about mid-October to April. The southwest winds tend to bring heavy rains, known as the monsoon season.

The wind and rain finally stopped as we were having dinner with Uptal's family. Several of them started talking about going tiger hunting and invited us to join them. Yes, today such an idea would bring howls of protest at most American dinner parties because tigers are so endangered. But back then in those areas of India, some people hunted wild animals for sport, including tigers, and would hang them on the wall as trophies. It was simply part of the culture.

They got their hunting rifles out, we all loaded into a couple of jeeps, and took off. It was pitch dark. We were in the mountains with no streetlights and no town or city within miles. This was can't-see-your-hand-in-front-of-your-face dark. It was still windy, and the narrow roads were flanked by large trees and tea plants on both sides. You could only see what was illuminated straight ahead by the headlights.

The hunters carried strong flashlights to look for tigers, which were too smart to show up. Apparently, tigers come out after rain, but not this time. Our travel came to a halt when we came to a large tree that had toppled during the storm, blocking the road completely, forcing us to turn back. Like the hunters we were disappointed, but the tiger hunting trip was nonetheless exciting to us.

After finishing breakfast the next morning, we toured the tea factory and learned how the tea leaves were processed. Tea estates made up of many tea gardens had their own brand of tea, similar to how a winery creates its own brands of wine from its vineyards. Tea from Darjeeling is considered by many—then and now—to be the best. Darjeeling, which is located only about seventy miles from my town Jalpaiguri, is surrounded by tea plantations that produce the prized, light-colored, floral-smelling tea. Around 25 percent of India's total tea output comes from Darjeeling.

Being at the tea garden brought back nostalgic memories of the train to Darjeeling, which was so small it was referred to as the Toy Train, and it ran on the Darjeeling Himalayan Railway's narrow-gauge track that was only a yard wide. The coal-and-steam-powered engine would slowly chug up the seven-thousand-foot high mountain. At the top of the mountain is the *Ghoom* (sleep) railway station. After the toy train passed Ghoom, it navigated a steep descent into Darjeeling via the Batasia Loop, a spiral railway considered one of the greatest engineering achievements in Darjeeling history.

The Batasia Loop area is famous for its scenic beauty, which back then you experienced up close as the trains were mostly open on all sides except for having a roof. Fog and clouds would envelope the open train blocking the view, then suddenly the train would come out into the blue sky and the mountains. This was fascinating to us.

When I was a boy, *Ghoom* was considered the highest railroad station in the world. It is still the highest railway station in India. We would hop on the train, ride for maybe fifteen minutes to enjoy the thrill and the beautiful scenery of the mountains, then hop off after.

When we finished touring the factory, we thanked Uptal and his family and said our good-byes. We were all eager to go home and had a long journey ahead. We were going to take a boat across the Teesta River to reach Jalpaiguri. These were not motorized ferries; boatmen used oars to propel the vessels from shore to shore. They were open—kind of like a giant rowboat—and carried not only human passengers but also goats, cows, and chickens. There were no life jackets, no chairs; you sat on the wooden boat bottom.

The last boat was just readying to leave when we arrived. Being the last ride across it was crowded, and initially the boatmen did not want to take us because it was already overly full. We begged them to take us, as did some of the other passengers. The boatmen finally relented, and we sailed across a calm river with small ripples. The tranquility of the afternoon was broken by the chirping of the birds and the sloshing sound of the oars hitting the water. The crimson sun setting behind the trees created a surreal backdrop to the end of our adventure.

My family had strongly objected to my going on the bicycle trip. I went anyway, but when we got closer to home, I worried I might suffer some punishment when I returned. But to my surprise, the family was simply happy that I was back safely and greeted me warmly. No punishment or even a cold shoulder.

After my return I took the practical examination, and about a month later got the results: I had passed the examination, and now it was time to select my future destination. I applied to different medical schools, and one of the medical schools in Calcutta called for an interview. I did not have good clothes for the interview, and we didn't have the money for me to go buy any, but a friend of mine who was my size was kind enough to lend me an outfit for the interview.

I was accepted at the R. G. Kar Medical School, which meant leaving my town and moving four hundred miles to Calcutta, which is where most of the medical schools in that region were located. As it happened some of my family also moved to Calcutta, where we rented a small house just after I got into medical school.

It was a wretched place, but that's all we could afford. It was long, like what they call shotgun homes in the American

South. There was a long row of rooms with verandas on each side, with probably six families renting the rooms. We had two rooms. My brother, sister, and I stayed in one room. Our older brother Dada lived with his wife in the other room. There was no electricity, no running water, no shower. In the mornings all the residents lined up to use the building's lone outdoor latrine. We shared the room with mosquitoes, cockroaches, and lizards. We hung mosquito nets every night primarily to avoid the bloodthirsty fliers—and not just because we didn't want itchy bites. Malaria was still a very prevalent disease in the early 1950s. One sixteen-year-old boy in that tenement got sick and went to the hospital. We were later told he had died of cholera. He was about my age.

One night my sister Kaku had apparently been too tired to hang the mosquito net, and a lizard dropped on her forehead from the ceiling. Her screaming woke us all up. I can only imagine her reaction if it had been a cockroach instead. She was deathly afraid of the scuttling insects, especially the flying ones, so we tried our best to keep them away from her. But despite our best efforts creatures still found ways to get in the house.

One of the duties that I shared with my older brother Kalu was to collect drinking water. We'd walk about fifty yards from the house to a metal pipe that protruded three feet out of the ground with a spigot on top. The water supply was turned on from a central location for two hours in the morning between six and eight o'clock. Everyone would place their buckets in a queue in front of the pipe. If we were late coming back, we might find our bucket at the very end of the line. And if our bucket did not reach the watering pipe before the water stopped running, we wouldn't have drinking water that day and would have to come back that evening when they turned the water back on for two more hours.

After placing my bucket I would accompany Kaku to the railway station where she would catch her train to her full-time job at a girls' school in North Calcutta. After finishing work she'd go to class at Calcutta University in the center of the city. She'd come back every evening dead tired. Kalu was an undergraduate and would tutor other students to earn some money for the family. Dada was currently unemployed and looking for a job.

Some people are confused as to whether to call the city Calcutta or Kolkata. There's a story behind those names that goes back to British rule when they changed the name to Calcutta. In the Bengali language the city has always been called Kolkata, the name of one of the three villages said to have become the modern city. In 2001 the government of West Bengal decided to officially change its capital city's official name back to Kolkata to reflect its original Bengali pronunciation. Most people comfortably switched between the Bengali and Anglicized pronunciation and spelling. However, some businesses and organizations stuck with Calcutta such as the Calcutta Electric Supply Corp. and Calcutta University. Since the events related in this book occurred prior to 2001, and it is in English, I've used Calcutta.

Our rental home was in South Calcutta and my medical school in North Calcutta. Just as there is a significant demographic and cultural difference between, say, East Los Angeles and West Los Angeles, the same is true of Calcutta's northern and southern areas. North Calcutta is an older area that was developed first and is known for its century-old buildings, most reflecting European styles of architecture, and narrow lanes. South Calcutta has more modern architecture.

It took a train, a bus, and a fair amount of walking to get to North Calcutta from the southern end of the city. And transportation in India wasn't comfortable like commuter transportation is in the States. Those trains and buses were packed like sardines. Not only are such conditions physically uncomfortable, they are also a perfect environment to spread illnesses.

One night I woke up with severe pain on the right side of my chest and had difficulty breathing. I woke up my sister, and at first she thought I was pretending—which I did do a lot—and told me to turn onto my other side and go back to sleep. But I was in genuine, severe distress and couldn't sleep. The next morning my older brother Kalu, who was ever so helpful, took me to the local general practitioner. I was so sick and out of it I had no recollection of what had happened. Kalu later told me that I was extremely weak and had difficulty walking and even sitting down on the way to the doctor, even though his office was nearby. Kalu finally took me to the professor at my medical school on the advice of our family practitioner. Because I was a medical student I had a much better chance to get in the hospital and have my professor take care of me. With much difficulty I managed the five-minute walk to the train station.

That was a life-threatening ride. I had to take the same train and the bus I took every day to school. It was office time and the train seemed even more crowded than usual, but somehow I managed to hang onto the rod of the train with a toehold on the step, hanging outside the train. The pain got worse as the train took off, and I had another spasm of chest pain and could barely take a breath. Even though it was only a fifteen-minute ride, it felt like an eternity. The train was wheezing by large, very high electrical posts, and I thought I was going to hit one of them any moment. I was dizzy, sweaty, and weak and thought for sure that I was going to fall off the train. Being young and having a strong will saved me from tragedy.

When we finally reached the station, we had to then walk five agonizing minutes to the bus stop. Once again, I rode outside, clinging to the bus while in horrible pain. The conductor stopped every three or four minutes to pick up passengers, so each time I had to get off and stand aside to let people on. After what felt like forever, we reached the professor's house where he had an office. My brother told him I was a new student and in great distress. He examined me and diagnosed me with tubercular pleurisy, which affects the lining of the lung and can be caused by bacteria and viruses as well as environmental substances. Unlike tuberculosis, which is caused by a specific bacterium infecting the lungs that causes symptoms such as coughing, weight loss, and spitting up blood, with pleurisy you might run a fever for a short time. But mostly you just have pain.

The professor announced he needed to admit me to the hospital. Unfortunately, though, it was a fifteen-minute walk to reach the hospital and each breath I took felt like a knife in my chest.

I was placed in the general ward. There were thirty beds, a common bathroom, and little privacy. I became a teaching case for the students and house officers, who all listened to my lungs with their stethoscopes, the deep breaths tiring and painful. But I let them do it since they were learning from me. The students were listening to the pleural rub, which sounds like squeaky leather, a characteristic of pleurisy.

My sister and my brother would visit me with home-cooked food and medicines. The patient or family was responsible to get any medicine prescribed by the doctor, and at one point I ran out. But then neither my brother nor my sister came to see me for several days. The doctors were asking where my medicine was and were not happy that I didn't have any. When my sister finally came to visit me with food and medicine, I was very angry with her. She timidly told me she and my brother hadn't wanted to face me until they got paid and could afford to refill my prescriptions because they were very expensive. Being seventeen and sick I did not comprehend how difficult this was for my siblings. But now in retrospect I feel so heartsick for the position they were in.

Although pleurisy is not as disabling as TB, it would still take me a long time to recover, and I would end up staying in the hospital for four months, forcing me to postpone medical school until the following year. Despite my long convalescence, the pain lingered, but that didn't stop me from socializing. After lunch—the hospital food was terrible—some of us would gather on the veranda and enjoy ourselves with conversation and lots of laughs. Eventually it occurred to me that all the laughing might be exacerbating the pain. I stopped joining the group, and within a week my pain disappeared, and I was discharged. My primary care physician told me that I should not commute and instead should stay in the dorm.

That sounded fine, but there was one problem: who was going to foot the bill for that?

Have Stethoscope Will Travel

After I fully recovered, I was readmitted to the school and on doctor's advice I was also given a room in the dorm. I was having difficulty paying for my school and dorm fees, so I applied for the Refugee Scholarship that was being offered to the needy students whose families belonged to East Pakistan, now Bangladesh.

I was eligible for the scholarship because of events that occurred in the aftermath of the partitioning that occurred after India gained independence. Many Hindus who fled to West Bengal came with little more than the clothes they were wearing. In an effort to help, the Indian government began a scholarship program for needy families who came to West Bengal after the partition. I qualified for the scholarship because we came from East Bengal. My uncles, aunts, and cousins had fled the mayhem with only the shirts on their backs. To save their lives they left their houses, properties, jobs, and businesses. That was the good news. The bad news was how difficult it was to actually secure the scholarship. After applying we didn't get a response. We repeatedly contacted the office, trying to coax, cajole, or compel someone—anyone—at the scholarship office to tell us the status of my application. Not only was there a lot of red tape when it came to grants, it helped if you knew the right people who could process your application.

Finally, the stars began to align. My sister had a friend who worked in that government office. And my family had also approached a member of the state assembly to ask for help. Between their respective efforts, I finally received the scholarship. To me it seemed like a windfall; it not only covered my tuition, room, and board, but there was enough left over to help my family financially and give me a little pocket change. My father instructed me to send all the extra money to him in Jalpaiguri, and he would then send me any cash I might need.

Even though the scholarship was approved, it was going to take several months to get the money, so my family and I needed to figure out a way to cover our expenses until then. The answer came from a fellow patient. He occupied bed nineteen, so we called him Oonish, which is Bengali for nineteen. After the hospital discharged us, we kept in touch. He had come from Bangladesh literally in tatters. He was single, had no possessions, and lived in a glorified camp. But he was also a very kind and helpful man. He had secured a job, and when he learned of my financial dilemma, he offered to tide me over until I got the scholarship money.

I discussed his generous offer with my family, and we accepted his gift on the condition he promised to accept repayment. In the end, he adamantly refused to take the money back, and for many years we maintained a cordial relationship. But as happens when life takes you down different roads, we lost track of each other. I will never forget his kindness and what it meant to me and my family.

At the beginning of the month, the postman came to my dorm—which was actually more like a youth hostel than a dorm on an American campus—and distributed money orders to my three roommates from their families. I never received a money order, which would sometimes make me a little dispirited. But I understood my family needed the money more than I did, so I learned to make do.

For example, I never bought a textbook while in medical school. They were far too expensive. I didn't buy a medical book until I started my practice years later. But one of my relatives, Debeshda, a physician who had helped me get into medical school, had given me a book on anatomy. That was the only textbook I had with me at school. Since they housed four students to a room, I could study whatever books my roommates were not using, be it pharmacology, physiology, or whatever. I suppose the library had those books available too, but I didn't like going to the library either.

While I might not have bought a book during my entire student career, I did spend money on other things. Some of my friends wore nice clothes. I liked good clothes too and wanted to look nice. I would write to my father and ask him to send me money, saying I needed it for a textbook. Then I would use it to buy clothes. I considered it a harmless white lie. I did not like to study, so I played some soccer on my dorm's team for intermural competitions.

My small indulgences and extracurricular activities were enjoyable, but my main focus throughout college was my dream of becoming a surgeon. However for a while it seemed I might be practicing a very different kind of medicine. I graduated from medical school despite my convoluted studying habits. As a custom there were no graduation parties.

In the United States medical school graduates do an internship, which is basically an apprenticeship in a hospital, where young doctors receive supervised, hands-on training, then progress to a residency, which is where they work in their specialty. In the UK, India, and some other countries, they call it a house officership.

In India we had very little choice deciding our specialty; the school decided that based on our marks in the subjects. They determined I should be in pediatrics, so after graduation, I did my pediatric house officership in my medical school. The house officers are also divided into different levels according to seniority. They are taught and supervised by the attendings and also receive a meager monthly stipend.

The system had junior and senior house officers, each rotating for six months. The junior would become the senior house officer after six months. All the branches of specialties had a registrarship following the completion of the senior house officership—except for pediatrics. For some reason, it did not.

We were supervised by the seniors, the resident medical officer (RMO), and our professors of pediatrics. Our duties included admitting the patients, doing history and physical, collecting blood and other body fluids, and advising the families. We had to bring the samples to the laboratory and examine them ourselves, which was done manually using rudimentary instruments. The final result would be checked by the pathologist. We had to present the cases to the professors and discuss different aspects of the cases. We also had to see outpatients.

We had a policy of admitting all patients needing hospitalization including private patients from our professors. When we ran out of beds, patients would be put on the floor or out on the verandas. There was only one pediatric floor, which was usually treating more than fifty patients at a time.

The pediatric unit had a smorgasbord of patients: congenitally deformed patients, cardiac valve problems, heart failure, and respiratory problems were common conditions. The overwhelming majority of patients suffered from tubercular meningitis, gastroenteritis, and thalassemia.

In my own experience many TB meningitis patients presented as gastroenteritis. These meningitis patients were very sick.

Another vexing problem was kwashiorkor, a condition caused by a lack of protein caused by severe malnutrition, a result of poverty. Later on it was also known as Harold Wilson Syndrome, named after the British Prime Minister who denied food for the starving Biafran children during the Biafran/Nigerian war in the late 1960s. Jamaican pediatrician Cicely Williams introduced the term kwashiorkor in a 1935 Lancet article, two years after she published the disease's first formal description. The name is derived from the Ga language of coastal Ghana, translated as the sickness the baby gets when the new baby comes, referring to how an older child develops the condition after it is weaned so a younger sibling can be breast fed. The lack of regular nutrition from breast milk often results in the malnutrition.

The syndrome manifests itself with a protruding abdomen from accumulation of fluid as well as an enlarged liver. The face and other parts of the body look emaciated, black hair becomes blondish. and the skin becomes lighter in color. Our kwashiorkor patients came from the nearby shanty towns or bustees. It was more a politico-social disease. They were refugees from East Pakistan (now Bangladesh), who'd arrived destitute, with only the clothes on their backs. The fledgling Indian Government, just out of the British Rule, could not help them too much. We used to admit these desperately malnourished kids mostly from the outpatients and get them better with proper nutrition, only to have them return later again malnourished. Fortunately, India has moved forward, and today kwashiorkor is a disease of the past.

Thalassemia was another common problem. India has a prevalence of thalassemia, which is a hereditary condition caused by abnormal hemoglobin. It is more common in West Bengal and the surrounding areas than in other parts of India. The Indian system of marriage within the same caste and same ethnic group may be perpetuating this disease. Counseling for the prevention of thalassemia is not readily available in rural areas of India. The severity of the condition depends on the type of the hemoglobin.

A son of my brother's friend had a major problem with

thalassemia. He needed frequent intravenous iron infusions, which were not available in India at that time. I continually sent intravenous iron from the United States. I also used to consult with the professor of hematology at the Tufts Medical Center regarding the treatment. She agreed with the treatment the patient was receiving in Calcutta. Unfortunately, he died in his twenties from sepsis. As his health failed the despondent patient said he did not understand why his parents had allowed him to be born. It was a very profound statement. Of course, there was no premarital or preconception counseling at that time in India.

Once I finished my house officership, I desperately—and quickly—needed to earn money, not only for me but also for my family. I didn't care if it was with an established practice or a company position.

One of my senior colleagues, Dr. A. K. Bose, had built a busy general practice near our college. His "office" was a chamber in a local drug store that provided him a working space and medical supplies, a usual custom at that time. One day Dr. Bose was called to help a man who had fallen on the street. Dr. Bose maneuvered through the crowd that was gathered around the man, who was complaining about pain in his right shoulder. Dr. Bose diagnosed a shoulder dislocation. While the man was still on the street and as the crowd watched, Dr. Bose reduced the dislocation with the help of one of the pharmacists. The injured man felt immediate relief and was very grateful.

The passersby who had watched Dr. Bose perform the reduction were very impressed, and the story of him treating the dislocation spread quickly by word of mouth. His fame attracted many new patients, and his practice became very busy. I thought that I could join his practice to cover patients during Dr. Bose's off hours. He had other thoughts. I learned the lesson that nobody wants competition, so needless to say he was not interested.

One of my classmates, Sumit Das, was working in the Community Hospital, which was founded in 1913 by some business magnates. The hospital's original mission was to provide affordable medical facilities to the community. It is still open today. At the time I was there, the hospital was run by board members called ministers.

My medical school's professor of cardiology, Dr. Mukherjee, was also the head of the Community Hospital's cardiology department. Sumit arranged a job for me with Dr. Mukherjee. I admitted patients, worked them up, and discussed the cases with Dr. Mukherjee. During that time Dr. Guha rejoined the hospital after returning from England where he had obtained an advanced surgery degree. Dr. Guha, who was the medical officer responsible for all admissions, had a good reputation as a doctor but wasn't always well-liked by the staff.

One evening a minister from the board was admitted. I worked him up, and my diagnosis was that he'd suffered a stroke. A ward attendant brought a handwritten note—the usual form of communication in those pre-digital days—from Dr. Guha saying he wanted to see me right away. The moment I walked up, he started to complain loudly about my poor workup; he did not believe the minister had suffered a stroke. I suggested that we go to a quiet place away from the patients and visitors; we did, and I stood by my original diagnosis. He did not appreciate that at all.

The following day Dr. Mukherjee asked me about the incident with Dr. Guha, and I recounted exactly what had happened. Dr. Mukherjee agreed with my diagnosis. Even so, the board sent a note to Dr. Mukherjee suggesting that he take formal action against me. Dr. Mukherjee replied that he was not going to take any disciplinary action but acknowledged that the board might do so. He advised me not to fight the board because I couldn't win. He found me a job at the Calcutta Medical College and the Hospitals in the Pediatric Department.

While there I heard that some friends had found jobs with the Indian Railways. Apparently, those positions were easily available, probably because some were located in the jungle where the railways were laying new tracks. I applied and then stalked the medical director every week to find out if I had gotten the job, and every week he'd tell me my name hadn't come up. Even though I needed the job and had not gotten the job yet, I was bold enough to ask him not to place me in some remote jungle.

Finally, my name came up, and I got the job. The terms of my employment included a fairly good salary, a house, and a first-class train pass.

Even better, I was not assigned to a jungle. I was posted in Kharagpur, which is about eighty-five miles west of Calcutta. Kharagpur was established as a railway junction back in 1898. According to area lore, the locals were initially afraid to travel by train, fearful the nearby bridge would collapse as the cars traveled over it. Plus, there were no separate seating arrangements for different castes and religions. But negative attitudes toward the railways started slowly changing when the company started hiring local men and gave free train rides and a blanket.

The strategy worked, and people embraced the railways, making Kharagpur a main railway hub. The city is also home to the very well-known Indian Institute of Technology, which was founded in 1950. This was the first of its kind in India and produced many graduates who occupy many high academic posts and lofty positions in multinational companies all over the world.

Before getting the railroad position, one of my classmates had mentioned that American hospitals were seeking doctors to fill positions. At the time the United States was an enigma to me. Years earlier I had been at a friend's house, and they had a copy of an American magazine called *Life*. I looked through it and saw pictures of beautifully manicured lawns, spacious houses, and a blurb saying that each family had two cars. I didn't believe it and dismissed the notion as fake news. That kind of prosperity seemed impossible and preposterous.

But the idea of going to the United States as a young doctor appealed to me, in part because I had always wanted to travel abroad. I am fascinated with seeing new places, meeting people, and absorbing local cultures. My desire to see the world wasn't driven by financial gain. There was no consideration of making large sums of money in my family's class of society.

Initially, going abroad meant going to England. Regardless of your field, many people went to England to earn their degrees; some would come back, some stayed. Even though India was now independent, in the 1950s we remained largely under England's shadow since they had ruled us for two hundred years. We were still English, even though we were not, so I too wanted to go abroad to advance my education. But those who went to England enjoyed financial support, which I did not. So that was not an option for me—or so I thought until my friend told me about hospitals in the United States that were seeking physicians. Even if it was more like an internship than a permanent, full-time position, it sounded wonderful and exciting. But again, who was going to pay for such an indulgence?

Especially since—according to my friend—before you could apply to work at an American hospital, you needed to pass the Educational Council for Foreign Medical Graduates examination. I knew nothing about the ECFMG, and my friend didn't have any specific information either, other than his belief it would cost a lot of money, so he wasn't going to pursue it. I knew he was wealthier than I was—his family owned properties in Calcutta—so if he could not afford it, there was no way I could.

Discouraged, I put the ECFMG and thoughts of America out of my mind—until one day when I was at the Calcutta Medical College Library and found the Directory of Approved American Hospitals. I browsed through the book, admiring the pictures of beautiful hospitals and residential quarters. The book also listed the average salaries paid. It was all an eye-opener. I knew then that I needed to at least take the ECFMG and see what happened.

I got an application for the multiple-choice exam, which came with a booklet that provided some sample questions and answers. I found the questions to be very easy. I filled out the application, mailed it in, and hoped I would be allowed to take the examination. That was around early 1962. Not long after, I received a letter announcing I had qualified to take the test. I did not immediately start studying because I didn't know how or what to study. I knew what I knew. If the sample questions were any indication, I knew enough. The real issue was the venue.

The examination was to take place at the Grand Hotel in Calcutta, which was more a palace than lodging. For me and my friends, the Grand Hotel was someplace beyond our means and status, essentially making it out of bounds for us. We used to walk by the hotel, and at the front entrance always stood two sentries with rifles in hand, bayonets attached—very similar to the guards at Buckingham Palace as far as the pomp and circumstance, except they wore decorative turbans and scarlet red uniforms with gold buttons. Peeping inside, we could see the lobby and bar filled with foreigners, which we found somewhat intimidating. Had I possessed wealth and social status, I doubt I would have felt so out of place.

Ironically, for all the Grand Hotel's gilded history and reputation, it had distinctly modest beginnings. The original structure was a Sussex-style house owned by a man named Colonel Grand, who had lived there most of his life. In 1870 an Irishwoman named Mrs. Annie Monk bought that property at 13 Chowringhee Road and the next two homes at 14 and 15 as well to open a boarding house.

Around the time Mrs. Monk was establishing her business, an Armenian from Iran, Arathoon Stephen, arrived in Calcutta and opened a silversmith business at 19 Chowringhee Road. Over the years he became a successful, wealthy jeweler, and in the early 1900s he bought 16 and 17 Chowringhee Road and turned one of the properties into the Empire Theatre. After the theatre burned down in 1911, Stephen bought out Mrs. Monk and also acquired 18 Chowringhee Road to own the block. He developed that real estate haul into the Grand Hotel, an opulent, three-story, five-hundred-room upscale lodging with neo-classic architecture that featured a fountain in the lobby and a wood-paneled lobby elevator.

The Grand Hotel quickly became a popular meeting spot with Brit ex-pats living in Calcutta as well as with foreign visitors. It was especially known for its annual New Year's Eve gala that featured iced champagne, expensive gifts, and releasing twelve piglets in the ballroom. Anyone who caught a piglet could keep it, giving a new perspective to bringing home the bacon.

Arathoon Stephen died in 1927, but the Grand Hotel lived on until a typhoid fever outbreak killed six hotel guests, which was blamed on the building's drainage system, forcing the hotel to close in 1937. Hotelier Mohan Singh Oberoi leased the property the following year and reopened the hotel in 1939, renaming it the Oberoi Grand. Different name, same attraction and reputation. During World War II about four thousand soldiers were housed there, and there always seemed to be parties and festivities occurring.

By the 1950s when I came to Calcutta, the Grand Hotel was a landmark. It was painted white and covered the entire block. Colonnaded verandahs and balconies on the upper floors were very reminiscent of British colonial times. And since it was located in the center of Calcutta's social and entertainment district, it maintained the aura of prestige, the lodging of choice for Indian royalty, foreign heads of state, and internationally known actors and writers.

What's interesting is that it remains one of modern Kolkata's premier hotels, where guests can sit on a balcony overlooking the courtyard and swimming pool while watching the sunset over the city.

However, I was not a worldly guest. I was a young physician who came to the Grand Hotel to take a test, waiting outside the building alongside many other hopefuls, who did not include anyone I knew. Everyone was speaking fluent English, was well-dressed, and looked confident. They had come from all over India as well as areas outside the country. I felt conspicuous and out of place and almost left without taking the examination. Fortunately, I stayed despite my discomfort.

It was a multiple-choice examination, and I had never taken one before. But the test wasn't quite as easy as the sample questions had suggested. In fact, it was rather difficult; the nurses would not have been able to breeze through it as I'd previously dismissed. Except for a one-hour break, I did not lift my head for six hours. Some questions I did not recognize at all. For one section, the examiner read from a book, and we had to write down what she was reading—not easy as her accent was difficult to decipher. It impressed me that they provided us with a sponge soaked in water to moisten our fingers to turn the page, so we wouldn't lick our fingers. I still do not lick to turn pages.

I finished the test and exited the hotel, resigned to not passing. Typically, after taking the test you would send for job applications from the American hospitals. But I did not. What was the point? Instead I ended up working for the railways, which from the start was not the best situation.

When I arrived in Kharagpur, there were no living quarters for me as they'd promised, so the company put me up in the first-class waiting room of the railway station. It might have been a good place to wait for a train but wasn't ideal for lodging. After a week and multiple requests, I finally secured my room, if you could call it that. It was unfinished and still under construction. There were bricks, cement, and other building materials strewn everywhere. The unit was like a garden apartment—which is partially below ground level—with the windows high up. If I wanted water, I had to go outside the building to get it. There was no electricity; nor do I recall having a proper bathroom. I slept on the floor on a blanket. I was a long way from the Grand Hotel.

One night voices woke me up to find two people peeping through the window. After I made a lot of noise, they left, but that scared me. And to top it off, I also got a bill for my stay in the first-class waiting room.

I told the medical director about all my problems. He told me not to pay the waiting room bill and promised to see if he could secure me a better room. He apparently couldn't. I never got better lodging during my time with the railway, but at least I did not have to pay the waiting room bill. Overall the medical director of the hospital was not very nice to me.

I was first posted in an outpatient clinic, then not long after they transferred me to another clinic. Most of the patients were South Indian and spoke Telegu. I did not understand them that well, but I managed. One day a patient approached me with a form. When I unfolded the piece of paper, I found a two rupee note inside. Assuming the applicant had made a mistake, I tried to give him back the money. The man begged me to keep the money and sign the form, which said his wife had anemia. I refused to take the money and also refused to sign the form without first examining his wife, who was not there. He left bitter and unhappy.

The next morning my immediate superior called me into his office, like the principal summoning a student. He chastised me for causing a problem in the clinic the day before. It was clear the problem was my refusal to sign a form saying a patient I had never examined suffered from anemia. My superior let me know in an indirect but clear way that if I did not conform to how the system worked, I could find myself transferred far away.

I did not argue or even respond. But I was still transferred to another clinic that was crowded with patients, dirty, very noisy, and where I had very little help. And because the railways had not paid me yet, I had very little cash. So even though the food was not good and gave me diarrhea every time, I ate at the cheapest South Indian restaurant I could find.

It was not a good situation. Nor was it the medical career I had envisioned since my youth.

Fortunately, my time working for the railways proved mercifully brief. I returned to my quarters one day after work and found a letter addressed to me in Calcutta pinned to my door along with a note from my brother, Kalu. He was an extraordinary person who would go far out of his way to help people. He had come all the way from Calcutta to give me the letter but could not find me, so he pinned it to my door then went back home.

I opened the envelope and found I had passed the ECFMG. I was flabbergasted. Then elated. Then scrambling. By then it was April or May, which was so late for applying to United States' hospitals because the residency programs started in July. I went back to the medical college in Calcutta to consult the directory and sent off applications to different hospitals. Three or four of them replied with job offers, but only one hospital sent me a check for three hundred dollars towards the airfare. That money made the decision of where to go much easier.

I was on my way to Connecticut.

But to actually get there required so much to do in a short amount of time, it was literally a race against the clock. The residency program started the first of July, and it was already May. The hospital wanted copies of all my educational certificates, and the American consulate required a medical certificate from their designated doctor, a chest X-ray, and blood tests to issue a visa. The problem was Kharagpur was not a place where these things could be done. I kept sneaking away to Calcutta so I could complete the requirements.

Everything was coming along fine except the educational certificates. The hospital would accept a photocopy, but neither my friends nor I knew anything about making photocopies. Xerox had introduced the first photocopier three years earlier in 1959, but it was probably not widely used in India yet. I went to several photographic stores and finally found one that could take pictures of the certificates and give me the copies. I was happy with the proposal, but because the railways still hadn't paid me I had to borrow the money to pay for the photos of the certificates, which I mailed to the Connecticut hospital.

With that done I turned my attention to getting a passport, a process that normally took months, in part because the Criminal Investigation Department (CID), which is similar to the FBI, had to investigate the applicant and their family. Then the governor of the state died the day before my scheduled interview with the CID, so everything shut down in official mourning, and the date had to be changed. I was also having trouble buying my plane ticket because the airlines I contacted would not accept the check from the American hospital. They wanted cash or a personal check, neither of which I could provide. The bank told me they had to put a twenty-one-day hold on the check before they would release the funds. I went to the American consulate and talked to the consul who told me to go to Citibank's branch in Calcutta, and they would have to send the check back to the main office for processing. How frustrating. Remember, this was in the days when checks had to be mailed via snail mail; digital technology was just a science fiction dream back then.

Again, I could hear the clock in my head ticking and knew time was running short. I started seeing the glass half empty and was certain that I was going to miss my appointment. It was incredibly stressful, and I was feeling a little defeated at that point. Just when it seemed hopeless, a travel agent who had just opened his business was willing to accept the hospital check, and he also offered to provide us with transportation to the airport. And my sister Kaku was able to borrow some money from a friend to cover the remainder of the ticket price and some pocket money.

When we were interviewed by the CID agent, we explained that I was going to the United States, and I was on a tight deadline. We asked if he could expedite the matter, and he said he would try. He kept his word, and my passport arrived in time. He was an honest man and expedited the matter without any gratuity. I was even more happy than I was relieved. I was finally ready to roll—almost. It was now the end of June, and I was never going to make the first day of the program on July 1st. I sent a telegram to the hospital, requesting a two-week extension for my arrival. The hospital was kind enough to agree.

Now that it was assured I had a ticket and a job waiting for me in Connecticut, there was a lot of excitement among my friends and family, who all came to celebrate at our house. The thought of leaving seemed unreal and surreal. Nobody in my family had ever gone abroad or flown in an airplane. Everyone just stayed. Although my brother the schoolteacher had received the Fulbright Scholarship several years earlier, he could not raise the money to go to the States.

I still needed to buy some clothes, including a suit and tie, which meant I had to learn how to make a knot. One of my sisters imagined I would be going to formal dances like she had seen in movies. Someone else observed I would have to learn how to use silverware. It was such an unknown I might as well have been going into outer space.

Once everything was in place, I paid a final visit to the railway clinic to officially resign. I explained to the medical director that I was going to work at a hospital in the United States. He wasn't particularly supportive, warning that I should think things out carefully before leaving because America was very expensive, and my meager pay may not be enough to live there. I thanked him for his concern then asked for my paycheck. I was preparing myself for him to not pay me because I hadn't been there a full month. To my surprise he sanctioned the payment but said it might take a few months to get the check. I should have been so fortunate. It would take a year and multiple trips to Kharagpur by my ever-helpful brother Kalu and my sister Kaku, who helped the family a lot, to finally get the check owed me.

The days passed quickly, and soon the time arrived for me to leave. I wore my suit and tie and carried a small suitcase, the size of today's carry-on bag. I had packed lightly because I didn't own much. Walking out of our home, I double-checked to make sure I had my passport, visa, airline ticket, and eight dollars, which was all I was allowed to carry outside the country. At the time India was not yet open to many outsiders, and the government wanted to keep their currency in the country. Before leaving I had to exchange about thirty-eight rupees to get the US eight dollar allowed amount.

The lane to our residence was too narrow for the transport, so I had to walk to the main street. My mother and some of my siblings accompanied me to the car. Three of my brothers rode with me to the airport; the rest said good-bye there. As we drove away I saw tears in my mother's eyes, and one of my sisters was sobbing.

When we reached Dum Dum Airport—today called Netaji Subhas Chandra Bose International Airport—it was a sea of people. Many of my friends showed up to see me off, several carrying bouquets of flowers, which was the custom then. They all asked me to write to them.

After going through the immigration process, which was minimal, they directed me to board the plane. In those days friends and family could come almost to the tarmac. After saying good-bye to everyone, particularly my family, I got onto the plane and sat down in my seat, which was an unbelievably exhilarating experience. A short while later the plane sailed away like a cloud in the sky, leaving my beloved Calcutta in the distance.

While I was writing this book, my sister told me that she and another sister sat on the roof of our house around the time my flight was to depart. They watched a plane fly overhead and believed I was on it. Hearing that was sobering and brought tears to my eyes, especially since one of those siblings had passed away recently. Looking back, I am struck now by how the awareness I would be leaving my parents and siblings behind for many years was lost on me in the excitement of my pending journey.

The trip from Calcutta to the United States was long and arduous. After a short stop in Bombay, we boarded a BOAC Airlines plane. On that flight I had a window seat and was delighted to gaze out at the world below. I admired the dark-blue hue of the night sky, the stars bright and so close to my window I felt that I could almost touch them. The stars brought me a message of a new horizon, of a wide-open world. When the stewardess offered some soft drinks, I didn't know what to choose, so she gave me a glass of ginger ale. That was the first soft drink I had ever tasted.

Today people fly wearing sweatpants and flipflops, but in 1962 flying was still a more formal affair. People dressed up as if going to church. Smoking was also allowed, so the air on the plane got stale and musty very quickly. The BOAC stewardesses looked smart in their crisp uniforms and were always attentive, even to those of us in the back of the plane flying economy.

The plane leapfrogged from Bombay to Karachi, Beirut, then Cairo. We arrived in Egypt during the early morning, with a large crimson sun rising in the east. As I had at every previous stop, I disembarked to venture into the transit lounge. When I came out of the plane, the hot air hit me. Even after growing up in India, this heat was fierce. Not many other passengers came to the lounge, so I sat down by myself. The tall, dark, and burly waiters kind of scared me. I ordered a lemonade and drank it with relish then hopped back onto the plane for the next leg of the journey, which was a stopover in Rome.

The plane was full of young faces going abroad to advance their education and life. Once we had flown into daylight, we milled around inside the plane, talking to anyone and everyone about where we were going and what we'd be doing. It was so exciting and invigorating.

Finally, after more than thirty hours of travel, we arrived at the airport in New York, and I stepped into a new world and a new life.

Welcome to the Emerald City

After what seemed like waiting a long time in my new alien environment, Mr. Kelly finally returned. He pulled his car to the curb, and after I tossed in my suitcase and got settled in the car, we drove off, leaving the bustling airport behind. During the ride we talked about different things. I am sure he did not understand my accent that well. I also had difficulty understanding his. But we managed. The ride to the hospital was so enjoyable and this new world I saw as we passed by was so pleasurably different with beautiful, well-kept roads lined by nice houses. The green pastures visible through the trees bordering the road were more bucolic than I expected.

When Mr. Kelly dropped me off at the hospital, a courteous staff member greeted me and escorted me to my room, which was cozy and comfortable—a far cry from my lodgings with the railroad. The single bed had clean sheets, a light blanket, and pillows—no mosquito net needed. There was also a desk with a table lamp, a telephone, a closet. The brightly lit bathroom was spic and span with no smell. No buckets or mugs to be seen anywhere. Instead of having to bathe using water dripping from a pipe, there were proper showerheads. Having your own bed, having a clean, disinfected bathroom—these are things most Americans take for granted. For me it was like being in Oz.

I learned quickly it was going to take time to adjust to the social and cultural norms. For example, in India I took showers wearing a lungi, which is a wrap-around garment that covers the lower body. No such deal here. I had to go right into the shower with no clothes on, which I found very embarrassing even though I was alone in the bathroom.

After showering and getting dressed, I emptied my suitcase and hung my clothing in the closet. Having just a few items in the closet seemed to magnify my meager possessions. Then I carefully hid my passport, the ECFMG certificate, and the remaining $6 of my spending money in a secure place.

There was a knock on the door. My visitor introduced himself as another house officer from Calcutta, then he welcomed me and invited me to have dinner in the residents' kitchen. I was hungry and happily accepted his offer. I enjoyed a hearty Indian meal and met more house officers, who were all very friendly, welcoming, and helpful.

I was eager to call back home so my family knew I had arrived safely. We did not have a phone in our house, but the family of my classmate Shyama, who we called Sam, did and he would convey the message to my family. I asked the other residents how to call India, and they advised me to dial the hospital operator who would help me. After finishing my dinner, the first thing I did when I returned to my room was to call the hospital operator. She did not know who I was since I had just arrived, and said she needed to call me back, so I hung up and waited while she confirmed my residency. When the operator called back, she welcomed me to the hospital then connected me with the international operator, who explained she would call me back with the time I would be connected to my friend in India. Calling overseas took a telephonic village in the 1960s. The process was completely new to me, and I was very worried that the international operator would never call me back.

We are now so used to being able to call anywhere in the world on our cell phones it seems like ancient history having to go through operators because there were no direct telecommunication lines from Connecticut to India. Calls were connected from New York to London to Sydney through underwater cables. Then it was overland transmission from Sydney to Calcutta. If the wind was blowing toward Calcutta, the connection would be great. But when the wind blew towards Sydney, you could hardly hear anything.

To my pleasant surprise and immense relief, the operator did call me back. After what felt like several anxious hours, even though it was mere minutes, the operator connected me with Sam. We were so excited to talk. I told him all about my trip, my experience at the New York airport, described my amazement about all the young people kissing and holding hands in public. The operators in Calcutta were eavesdropping, and I could hear them chuckle. We talked for forty minutes, and before hanging up I made sure that he would let my family know as soon as possible that I had called. I fell asleep happy and content.

The next morning one of my newfound friends took me to the cafeteria for breakfast. It was small, but what impressed me was its cleanliness. There were no flies, and all the food was covered. I had no clue about cafeteria etiquette, so I copied everything my friend did. There was a menu on the wall listing the options. The terms might as well have been written in Greek. Hamburgers, hot dogs, bacon, bagel, English muffin—so many of the food options were absolutely unfamiliar to me.

I picked up a tray then stood in the slowly moving line, which was very disciplined, with nobody trying to cut ahead of you. I pushed my tray along the tray slide, still studying the undecipherable menu. Toast sounded familiar, so I ended up ordering that and picked up a can of pineapple juice and a glass of water. Even though the food was free for the house officers, everybody still had to stop at the cash register so it could be rung up. The cashier was a young lady with blonde hair and blue eyes, which to me was unusual enough, but what surprised me the most was that she was smoking. Women in India generally do not smoke, so I concluded that she must not be well-mannered.

I sat down at the table and picked up the knife and fork. Traditionally Indians do not use cutlery for eating food; we prefer eating with our fingers. It is done neatly, and only the tips of the fingers are used. Or we would use a piece of flatbread to scoop food such as curry. It was a humbling experience learning to correctly use the knife, the fork, the spoon, and the napkin. Holding the fork in the left hand to steady the food so it could be cut with the knife in your right hand was initially cumbersome.

The napkin was another problem. We initially placed the napkin on the table. Gradually we learned that the napkin should be kept on your lap, used to wipe or blot your face to keep it clean, and then place the stained napkin back on your lap. We felt that was unclean. In India we washed our hands before and after eating, as we used our hands to eat, and we also washed our faces after the meal.

Then there was the matter of saying *excuse me* for reaching across the table or when leaving the table for a bathroom break. Because we never used those words back home, we had to make a conscious effort to remember that simple phrase. In the hospital cafeteria these manners were not strictly observed. However, going out to a restaurant or to someone's house as a guest was a much different matter. We did not want to be seen as rude. We did not want to be embarrassed in front of our colleagues and friends. We did not want to be ridiculed by a local asking why we didn't know basic manners. Every little thing which was taken for granted in our new country, was new to us. We were learning foreign attitudes, etiquette, and manners as we were trying to assimilate into the society.

When I asked my friend if there was somebody who would serve us tea, he laughed and explained that in American workplaces there were no servers. You had to get it yourself. I could not believe that I had to get the tea myself despite being a physician. Such a do-it-yourself system was a real culture shock—but not as much as discovering that after finishing the breakfast, I had to put away the tray myself. That was really a below the belt insult.

The day after my arrival, the nursing supervisor showed me around the hospital. I was surprised to see how clean the wards and rooms were. There was no smell. Trash was kept in trash bins, not strewn all over the place. All the patients were in beds; no families were sitting on the floor. There were no cats scrounging for food.

The nurses welcomed me with warmth and memorable friendliness, making me feel at home. I met the CEO of the hospital who came across as rather stern but still friendly. I also met some physicians, including Dr. Ghatak, who was the most senior resident among us, having already been there for a few months. He was a Calcutta boy but had attended a different medical school than me. He was tall, dark, and handsome with a good reputation in the hospital. When introduced, I used my full name, Amitabha Ghosh Roy. He told me nobody was going to be able to pronounce it or remember it; he decided to call me simply Dr. Roy. I quickly got used to it, and ever since then in America I have been known as Dr. Roy. I continued to introduce myself as Dr. Roy.

At the end of the tour, I was given my work schedule and also my uniforms. They were white tops with the buttons over the left shoulder and white trousers. I thought it was kind of funny that we had to wear such unseemly attire. Back home we wore our regular clothes. As excited as I was to get started, I was also feeling a bit overwhelmed. Not from the jet lag or being away from home but from the newness and the differences. Americans take cafeterias, showers, dressing areas, and lounge rooms for granted. They also don't give social norms a second thought; they come automatically.

On my tour of the hospital, I'd hear people constantly saying *thank you* and *nice to meet you*. I realized I would need to learn those niceties because they were expected. It did not come naturally. In India we don't say those things out loud; instead, we imply it by tone and body language. Many times during my first weeks working at the hospital in Connecticut, people would ask me: *Don't you know how to say please ... excuse me ... whatever?* Again, I did not like those comments. We were anything but rude or impolite. We were very respectful. Back home we did not have to say that. Nobody tried to find out why we did not say those niceties.

At the same time we got some laughs out of those niceties. After sneezing, a person would say *excuse me*, someone else would say *God bless you* to them, and the sneezer would say *thank you* in response. People would also say *excuse me* after burping. We used to laugh about it and always wondered why we had to do that.

Sometimes we would get mixed up. One day we were sitting at a table eating lunch. Some local friends were also at the table. One of us burped then said *thank you* instead of *excuse me*.

A local guy said, "At least he is learning." We burst out in laughter.

How ten thousand miles change everything. The food is different, how you eat is different, how you go to the bathroom is different, how you take a shower is different. And you even change your name. It was like being in an alternate universe.

The next morning my phone rang. It was the hospital operator who told me I needed to report to the business office. I assumed there was probably some paperwork I needed to fill out. But when I walked in, the accountant asked me if I had made a call to India. Still unconcerned, I told him I had. Then he announced that my telephone bill was $46—a dollar a minute—and I was expected to pay it. One of my friends told me that the phone calls were free in America. So much for phone calls being free. Walking out of the office, I felt sucker-punched, almost physically ill. I had no money, and my paycheck would not cover $46. Why hadn't I simply confirmed that calls were indeed free?

I was badly shaken at owing what to me was a king's ransom and couldn't stop thinking about it, trying to figure out what I was going to do. By the next day when I got another call from the business office, I was panicking. I was afraid they would rescind my position and send me back to India if I couldn't pay. I knew I had stayed on the phone for a long time—far longer than necessary to simply pass a message along to my family. How could I justify that? In my defense, during the entire phone call, I could not hear Sam half the time because of the poor connection. The wind had obviously been blowing the wrong direction that evening, which I would explain to the bookkeeper.

In the end I didn't have to defend myself at all. The bookkeeper informed me that he had talked to the telephone company, which had agreed to waive half the charge, and the hospital would absorb the rest. I thanked him profusely, feeling profound gratitude and palpable relief as if I'd been given a second chance to make the most of my time there. I was also very impressed with their compassion toward me and their willingness to help solve the problem caused by my ignorance.

A new day would start next morning, and I was eager to face it.

Different countries have different systems for educating and training doctors. In the United States there are generally three steps. The first is medical school, which is a four-year curriculum. Once you graduate from medical school, you are technically a doctor, although not yet licensed to practice on your own. Residency is the continued, hands-on training of a doctor at a hospital. First-year residents are called interns. Depending on the hospital's program, you can either spend that year learning different aspects of one specialty, say emergency medicine, or you can rotate through various specialties, the idea being to give young doctors a better sense of what specialty they want to pursue. Then starting in their second year of post-graduation training, residents focus solely on their specialty of choice.

The format of the residency educational program when I was in Connecticut was to rotate through the different clinical departments such as surgery, pediatrics, ob-gyn, etc. I was assigned to medicine first. We had to work up the new admissions, do a physical examination, and dictate the medical history. For all the interns from India, dictation was an unfamiliar task, it wasn't second nature, especially since I never liked to take notes or write things down. Instead I preferred to simply keep them in my head, which was often a challenge because on some days there would be five, six, or more admissions. The dictation stations were not where the patients were, so to dictate each history and physical one at a time meant I would have had to continually walk back and forth. I found that was not user-friendly, so my system was to talk to the patients and examine them one-by-one and then dictate all the results at once. Did I make mistakes once in a while? Unquestionably yes, but nothing that ever caused a problem.

My work also included making rounds in the morning on the assigned patients then discussing the nature of the illness and the investigations, interpretations, and treatment plans with the attending physicians, who in essence were our teachers. They were all patient, helpful, and friendly as they would take us through the different aspects of the cases. Rarely did any of them ever get angry or raise their voices. The attendings discussed cases in a very thoughtful manner and treated us as their equal.

It was such a different teaching approach from my past experience in India, where the attendings not only treated us not as knowledgeable but many of them were also very confrontational. But in the United States, if we did not answer a question correctly or did not understand something, the attendings would explain it and help us figure out the answer. That system encouraged us to study, participate in discussions, not be afraid, and learn. We worked much harder in America than we had in India, and most of the time it was with exponentially more pleasure.

Throughout the day there would be meetings with the attendings on different subjects. Some attendings were good, some not so good. It's the same in any profession. We quickly identified which attendings did not know much, although we still learned something from all of them because the system was so organized, so disciplined, and so educational. When I was back in India, I never imagined such a system existed.

Our schedule at the Griffin hospital had us on duty every other night and every other weekend, which seemed like a luxury. In India we are always on call. There is no such thing as weekends or nights off. I was slowly getting accustomed to the routine and to my new environment. It became easier to go to the cafeteria and eat. Spoken words became easier to understand. My accent was slowly softening so the personnel could better understand me. I started to enjoy hamburgers, hot dogs, and bacon, not realizing I was eating beef and pork, which we Hindus do not eat in India. However, necessity made me adapt.

I also noticed something interesting. Young schoolgirls in a special white uniform with red stripes were working in the hospital. Called candy stripers because their uniforms looked like a candy cane, they were volunteers who helped the nurses and also the patients. I learned the concept originated in 1944 at East Orange General Hospital in New Jersey, and by the time I arrived in America, the system was meant to encourage young women to become nurses, doctors, or healthcare workers. I thought it was a novel idea and wished there was a similar program in India.

Professionally, things were progressing beyond my expectations. I was also thriving on a personal level. I made friends easily and got along well with the other residents, physicians, nurses, patients, and all the hospital personnel. I enjoyed making rounds with the attendings, discussing cases, and bantering back and forth. Sometimes, I would correct the attending if I thought he was wrong, and if I was right, he would graciously acknowledge it. And likewise, if

I was wrong, the attending would correct me without blame or criticism, which helped me to learn and encouraged me to keep spreading my medical wings.

Not all of my compatriots were adjusting as quickly as I did. Homesickness can take many forms. For some it was missing family and familiar surroundings. For others it could be more basic. One of my classmates had a very hard time adapting to American food and almost left within a week of arriving because he missed his rice and curry. I didn't have any such problem. I just took what came. Trying to calm my classmate down, I told him: *Listen; just sit tight. You'll get used to it.* And he did.

For my part I wanted to explore. Specifically, I wanted to go to New York. Before leaving India that was the one place my family urged me to visit—New York is a big name everywhere. Back home the city was famous for the Empire State Building, the United Nations, all the skyscrapers, and the Statue of Liberty. Soon after arriving in Connecticut, I was already mulling over how to get there.

Then Romero, a lab worker from the Dominican Republic, solved the problem. He asked me if I wanted to go to New York. He and two of his friends—Andy, another hospital employee, and his girlfriend—were going to spend a weekend there, and if I was off, I could join them. The plan was to leave Friday evening after we all finished our shifts. Andy would be driving. I just had to share the expenses, and I would have to find a place to stay for the night. We would return separately. I would have to take the train.

Obviously, a hotel would be too expensive. But there was a much less expensive option. In the early 1960s Indian students, researchers, and physicians had started coming to the United States in growing numbers. It was a close-knit community, and I learned from others that it had become customary for those going to New York to look up Indian or Bengali names in the telephone white pages, call the number, introduce themselves, then request accommodation for however many nights needed. Nobody refused, and everybody was welcomed. The brother of a classmate of mine had given me a name of someone who lived in New York and told me to contact him. His name was Mr. Ranganathan.

I called him up and politely asked if I could spend the weekend at his place in New York; I would be arriving Friday night about nine o'clock and would leave on Sunday. Mr. Ranganathan did not hesitate to extend an invitation.

"No problem. We would be glad to have you."

I was very thankful and also relieved.

We got a late start the Friday we were leaving; everyone worked later than seven, Andy and his girlfriend did not arrive until after eight o'clock. He introduced his girlfriend, Jane, to us. I was most impressed with his shiny, long, burgundy-colored car. I was slowly learning the different car models people drove in America, and I thought it might have been an Impala.

Finally, we were all ready and got into Andy's car. I knew New York was not too far away in miles, but I did not know how long the drive would take. Andy told me we would not reach New York before ten o'clock. There were no smartphones back then, and I did not want to delay our travel by stopping to find a telephone so I could call Mr. Ranganathan and let him know about my delayed arrival. I convinced myself that ten at night would not be too much of a problem.

We were all in a good mood and having fun. The car radio was blaring. There was a steep downhill slope to reach the highway for New York. Being a Friday there was a lot of traffic on the highway. As we started going down the hill, Andy screamed. The brakes were not working, and the car was rapidly gaining speed. If Andy couldn't slow down or stop the car, we would surely crash. I was very scared. I did not want to die in America, especially before seeing New York.

Andy was trying very hard to stop the car, but nothing worked. The runaway car plunged onto the highway, but Andy skillfully avoided colliding with the other cars. He somehow maneuvered the car to the soft shoulder and slowed to a stop. Our mechanical difficulty was a major problem in many aspects. I was worried about Mr. Ranganathan. I assumed going to New York was now out of the question. I also wondered how we were going to get back to the hospital.

Andy and Jane left to find a gas station. Romero and I stayed with the car. He kept insisting that we would still be going to New York. It felt like Andy was gone for a long time, but when he reappeared, it was with his friend David, who happened to be a car mechanic. David had brought some tools, and between the two, they somehow fixed the brakes temporarily. I marveled at their Yankee ingenuity of repairing the car on the roadside. It was a completely new experience.

David advised Andy not to take the car to New York; we should get another car if possible. After David left, we all got back into the Impala. Andy cautiously drove to his house and picked up his mother's car. I was anxious about inconveniencing Mr. Ranganathan—someone I didn't even know nor had ever met—but didn't have the courage to ask Andy to drive me back to the hospital so I could avoid arriving late at my lodging. I also had a burning desire to go to New York.

    We all got into his mother's car and began our fateful journey. Andy took a different route and did not go down the steep incline. After driving for a little while, Andy realized that he was not going in the right direction. He had a two-way radio and called the local police station asking for directions to New York. I was gobsmacked that you could have a two-way radio, call the police, and get the directions from them. In my previous travels while in the United States, whoever I was traveling with would stop at a gas station and ask for directions, which might have been better. As the policeman talked I could tell Andy was having difficulty following his directions. GPS, which was ten years away from being developed, would have been very helpful.

    We stopped a few times for snacks. While the others eagerly consumed their food, I was more interested in enjoying the scenery; the mixture of light from the houses and the night's darkness added beauty to the trees, rocks, hills, and lakes we passed. The rhythmic music on the radio was soothing to the ears. Eventually I saw lit-up skyscrapers in the distance and felt a thrill; I was overjoyed to see the New York skyline.

    It took some time to find the street where Mr. Ranganathan lived. I believed it was in the Bronx, but none of us were familiar with New York neighborhoods. The roads were mostly empty, and I knew it had to be past midnight. I was shocked to see a little girl all by herself, nonchalantly roaming the street. She did not look afraid, but I was afraid for her. None of the others in the car paid any attention to her, and we kept driving.

After driving around a long time, we finally found his house. Andy, Romero, and Jane waited in the car to make sure Mr. Ranganathan was there. I rang the doorbell, the door opened, and he welcomed me to come in. I said goodnight to my friends in the car and thanked them. Now that we were in New York, we'd be going our separate ways.

I was shocked to learn it was close to two o'clock in the morning. I profusely apologized to Mr. Ranganathan for arriving so late and explained our mechanical debacle. He told me not to worry. His wife, Lakshmi, a beautiful lady, also welcomed me. When I came out of the bathroom after freshening up, I was surprised to see that she had prepared a plateful of Indian food for me even though it was so late at night; I was humbled by their hospitality.

The next morning I asked Mr. Ranganathan if he'd be willing to show me around New York. He gladly agreed. After a leisurely, tasty Indian breakfast—my first since leaving home—I was ready to explore. On the top of my list was the famous Empire State Building, then the tallest skyscraper in the world. That was the first place we visited. I did not realize you had to pay to visit the top floor. Mr. Ranganathan said that he would wait for me in the lobby. I thought he probably did not want to spend the money, so I offered to buy his ticket. It turned out he had an issue with heights; he said it made him dizzy.

As I was going up in the elevator, my stomach felt like it was getting sucked in. I'd never ridden an elevator that high before. That was an experience in itself. But nothing compared to walking onto the observation deck on the eighty-sixth floor and looking out and down at the spectacular view of the city: the Pan Am and Chrysler buildings, the skyscrapers, beautiful bridges, the rivers, the traffic below.

Seeing the awe in the faces of all the tourists around me on top of the city was an unforgettable moment. After spending some time voraciously absorbing all that I saw, I went back downstairs to where Mr. Ranganathan was waiting for me and excitedly told him about my superb experience. Thinking back on it now, I wonder how many times he had heard other visitors regale him with the same wonderment.

We went all around Manhattan, past the United Nations, through Times Square, alongside Central Park—uptown to downtown, East Side to West Side. Walking the streets of New York, I faced multitudes of people crowding the sidewalks, listened to the clamoring of honking cars, smelled the exhaust from buses, watched the throngs going into and coming out of the subway stairs. The din of the city took me back to Calcutta. I felt at home. I found the streets of New York City were pretty wide. Long buses, cars, taxis, bicycles, and motorbikes filled the streets. Throngs of people crowded the sidewalks, which were also very wide. I cannot describe the thrill that I, an Indian Bengali from a small town, experienced walking the streets of Manhattan. I was not looking at pictures on a postcard; I was physically touching the ground of the city. But as exciting, interesting, and novel as it was, the time had come for me to leave this impressive, one of a kind, vibrant city.

I returned to Connecticut by train, boarding at Penn Station. The train had many compartments and was much longer than the trains in India. The seats were not reserved, but the race to find a good seat was civil. People did not run over one another to grab a seat. In India when I was traveling back and forth to Calcutta from the railway hospital, I traveled in first class. But even those seats were not as wide and comfortable as my economy class seat here.

During the trip back to Connecticut, the images of New York still vivid, I recalled another train trip. After finishing our second year of medical school, Manik, Sam, and I took a trip to Delhi to see the Taj Mahal and other nearby places of pilgrimage. To pay for the trip I sold the anatomy textbook that my uncle had given me. I felt a little sad and sentimental about giving up the only textbook I had, but that was more than offset by my excitement over our planned vacation. We traveled by train, but it was an experience unlike any that American commuters could imagine. You had to carry your own mattress, pillows, and clothes in a large leather case that folded into a neat little suitcase, or you would just roll up the mattress with your necessities inside, secure it with a tie, then carry it. It was a long train ride, taking twenty-four hours.

I stayed with my brother, who was working in Delhi; Sam and Manik were staying with one of Sam's relatives. After spending a day sightseeing in Delhi, we went to Agra by train to see the Taj Mahal. Sam knew a Mr. Singh in Agra—the friend of a friend situation—and we decided to stay at his house even though Mr. Singh knew nothing about it. Communication was nonexistent. Most people, including Mr. Singh, did not have phones; letters were unreliable and if they actually arrived took many days. But in India during the 1950s, and maybe even today, it was not unusual to arrive at someone's door unannounced, to stay for a few days. The host will accept you without hesitation, but that didn't necessarily mean they were happy about it.

According to the plan, we arrived at Mr. Singh's. He opened the door and had no idea who we were. We introduced ourselves, and Sam explained our connection to him. We politely asked if we could stay a couple of nights at his place. Even today I cannot forget the shock on his face. He welcomed us in because you did not refuse a guest in India, but looking back now it's clear he was distressed, and I can see why. He was a man of meager means. He had a wife and three small children and only had two rooms. But he was a gentleman, polite, and so were his family. He treated us very courteously and apologized for not being able to give us Bengali food. As young men we didn't appreciate the depth of his hospitality.

When in Agra we traveled by bus or rickshaw. The first place we visited, of course, was the Taj Mahal, which was built by Emperor Shah Jahan in memory of his wife, Mumtaz Mahal. In essence it is a huge mausoleum built of translucent white marble. The construction started in 1632, took ten years and twenty thousand artisans to build, and in today's money would cost more than $800 million to construct.

The approach to the Taj Mahal is along a reflective tree-lined canal. The exteriors of the Taj are inlaid with intricate decorations, inlaid with precious gemstones like opals, lapis lazuli, and jade, giving stunning flashes of color against the white background. Stucco and paintings cover the exterior walls along with calligraphy of verses from the Quran and excerpts from Persian poems in black marble. Murals of herringbone inlays and mosaics of colored stones in geometric patterns along with abstract tessellations cover the exterior floors and surfaces. Another intricate work of art was the creation of marble screens, or *jalis,* by cutting delicate designs into the stone. The semiprecious stones were inlaid in the flowers, vines, and fruits decorating the marbles. The tombs of Shah Jahan and Mumtaz Mahal are located in the lower levels in the center, under the building's iconic dome. We were all so very impressed by its architectural beauty. The calligraphy was exquisite and was written with black color on white marble or white on black, making it vibrant. Unfortunately, many precious stones and gems were taken by the British soldiers leaving pockmarks on the beautiful marble.

Not too far from the Taj was Emperor Akbar's tomb, which was built in the early 1600s. It was as beautiful as the Taj but on a smaller scale. I liked the tranquility, the gravity, and the aristocracy that gave it a special character. Akbar built a township, Fateh-Pur-Sikri, for the royal palaces. In 1580 Akbar built a tomb to honor a Sufi Saint named Salim Chisti, who had predicted that Akbar would have a son. Akbar's son Jahangir was born and became the next emperor. This tomb was thought to be the first and finest example of Moghul architecture. Akbar abandoned Fateh-Pur-Sikri after a few years We also saw Buland Darwaza (Gate of Victory), a fifteen-story high sandstone gate with marble decorations that Akbar built to commemorate a military victory.

We had a great visit in Agra, and the memory of the Taj remains vivid even today. But it was time for us to leave for Delhi. We sincerely and profusely thanked Mr. Singh, and to this day I have never forgotten his family's extraordinary hospitality and warmth.

When we returned to Delhi, we visited the city's oldest monument, *Lal Qila* or Red Fort, which was also built by Shah Jahan, and the palaces inside it. In 1857 during the first Indian Rebellion for Independence, the British ransacked the place, broke down the walls, and looted the furniture from the living quarters. Most of the jewels and artifacts of the Red Fort were removed by the British and are now found in different attractions in London. The first Prime Minister of India, Pundit Jawaharlal Nehru, hoisted the Indian National Flag at the Red Fort (*Lal Qila*) on the night of August 15, 1947, when India became independent. Nehru gave his famous "A Tryst with Destiny" speech of independence there, a tradition that still continues.

> Long years ago we made a tryst with destiny ... A moment comes, which comes but rarely in history, when we step out from the old to the new, when an age ends, and when the soul of a nation, long suppressed, finds utterance.

We also visited the Qutab Minar, a five-story tower built in 1193 by Sultan Aibek immediately after the defeat of Delhi's last Hindu kingdom, and the famous Ashok Stambha, a twenty-five-foot pillar that is the national emblem of India. This pillar was built from 268 to 232 BC by King Ashok, made of wrought iron mixed with chemicals. The iron is rust proof and the subject of scientific investigations. At the top of the pillar are four lions and a chakra, or wheel. The four lions are the emblem of India and the chakra, representing progress, is in the center of the Indian National Flag.

After finishing our sightseeing in Delhi, we geared up for visiting the sacred pilgrimage sites. Our first stop was Haridwar, located on the shores of the Ganges., where there were many Hindu temples. People go there to take a dip in the Ganges, hoping to attain *moksha*, which is a Hindu concept about freedom from the cycle of life and death.

Attaining moshka is somewhat akin to the Christian concept of eternal salvation or the Buddhist concept of nirvana. Hindus believe that the soul passes through a cycle of successive lives, and its next incarnation is always dependent on how the previous life was lived. In a lifetime people build up karma—both good and bad, based on their actions within that lifetime—that affects their future lives and existences. People must take responsibility for their actions either within this lifetime or the next.

We did not want to take a dip in the Ganges, which was crowded with people swimming, bathing, and taking holy dips. There were huge crowds around the temples, and finding accommodations was overwhelming. As usual we were traveling with our mattress, pillows, and other belongings. We landed at a *dharmsala*, similar to a youth hostel. Rather than having individual rooms, it was a large communal hall where people spread out their mattresses on the cement floor next to all the other lodgers. There was no facility for food, but there were water taps. The worst part was you had to share the few available bathrooms with the other hundred or so people who had stayed overnight. Some of the bathrooms did not have any doors, and none were particularly clean.

We decided to visit whatever places we could and quickly return to Delhi. We went to another holy place a short distance from Haridwar called Rishikesh, which many people consider the yoga capital of the world. It's home to many ashrams where people can meditate and practice yoga. Since ancient times Hindu sages and saints have visited Rishikesh in search of higher knowledge, so it is considered one of India's holiest places for Hindus.

We crossed the Ganges River on the Lakshman Jhola suspension bridge, which first opened in 1929. It was built on the site Hindus believe the god Lakshman crossed the river on a bridge made of burlap. The aging bridge, which was designed for foot traffic but is regularly used by motorbikes, was closed in July 2019 because of fears it could fall, but when we were there it was still relatively new.

On the other side of the bridge, we walked along a path between the Ganges and the foothills of the Himalayas. This path was full of monks. Some were naked and covered with ash from head to foot, sitting in a lotus position and smoking ganja (cannabis); others were panhandling. We saw one monk standing on one leg, his arms extended overhead with hands folded in prayer. We were told he'd been in that position for days. An ash-smeared hand was sticking out of the ground holding prayer beads, with no visible person attached. The rest of him was probably ensconced in an underground hole. There were monks lying on a bed of nails, some not blinking their eyes for hours, others eating fire or running through the fire.

Despite the altitude, the air temperature was very hot. The more heated we got, the more inviting the flowing Ganges seemed; it practically called out inviting us to take a dip to cool down. There were concrete steps leading down to the water. Sam was a strong swimmer and loved the water. He took his shirt off, walked down the steps, and dove into the water. Seconds later he shot up out of the water screaming. I jumped into the water thinking something had happened to him then wanted to scream myself—the water was freezing. Turns out the Ganges's average temperature ranges between 50° and 60° F. The water was so cold because the Ganges is fed by melting snow on the Himalayas. A day later I developed laryngitis and could not speak for a week.

After visiting the holy sites, we went back to the dharmasala to pick up our luggage and then returned to Delhi. We spent a night in Delhi. Next day when we left for Calcutta, my brother accompanied me to the railway station and met my friends. While waiting for the train, he also helped us get some porters to carry our luggage. When the train arrived at the station, pandemonium broke out. Everybody was shoving each other out of the way to get into a compartment. The porters guided us through the throng into a compartment, where we somehow found seats, then placed our luggage on the overhead bunk. After the usual haggling over the porters' fee, they eventually left happy.

The trains were usually packed with people crammed in like sardines. You could not lie down during the almost twenty-four-hour journey to Calcutta, and you had to keep a close eye on your luggage and wallet, so it was nearly impossible to sleep. Riding the train was also somewhat romantic, looking out the window as it whistled by the villages, the fog-shrouded paddy fields, the mud huts in the distance, illuminated by the glow of kerosene lamps. It was beautiful to watch. When the train made a stop at some stations, it was almost musical to hear the hawkers selling tea, biscuits, or sweets. I remember those train rides with much nostalgia.

Back in Calcutta we returned to our school dorm and showered, ate a meal, then fell into a deep and satisfied sleep.

The compartment of the train back to Connecticut was full of schoolboys and their chatter, which roused me from my memories. I was the only dark-skinned person in the car, and in my mind I assumed they probably wondered why I was there. But nobody bothered me or paid much attention to me at all. From time to time I would hear some of the boys shout out repeatedly a word that sounded like *re six*. I did not know what that was or why they were yelling it so much.

From the train station I took a bus to my hospital. Despite the busy weekend, I felt energized. The first thing I did once back in my room was write a letter to my father about my trip to New York. Like a little boy, I eagerly described all the places I had visited and experienced, like the heart-stopping ride to the top of the Empire State Building and the aggregations of so many nationalities speaking their native languages. I shared my pride in seeing India's national flag flutter with the flags of other countries at the United Nations and my amazement at the massive subway system and long buses. I included many postcards of New York in the envelope with my letter.

I also shared my fascination at how nobody jostled aggressively for seats in the buses or trains nor did anyone have to ride buses or trains by hanging onto the outside of the train car. And lastly I told my family about Mr. and Mrs. Ranganathan's hospitality and requested they pass along my appreciation to the friend in Calcutta who had given me the Ranganathans' contact information.

The next day, Monday, I was back at work. I told the doctors and the nurses about my exciting experience of visiting New York City. One of the doctors asked if I had gone to see the Yankees-Red Sox game. I had not a clue what they were talking about. Later I realized he was talking about a baseball game, and I finally understood what the boys on the train had been shouting.

Red Sox!

Medical Culture Shock

As is inevitable at a hospital, I experienced my first tragedy. Late one afternoon a patient in his sixties was admitted. He was vomiting large amounts of blood, probably was bleeding from engorged and broken veins in his esophagus. His blood pressure had also dropped. He had previously been diagnosed with cirrhosis of the liver. Being in pediatrics, I never encountered a bleeding cirrhotic patient in India, so I didn't know quite how to handle the situation. The incidence of alcoholic cirrohsis was quite low in India. The attending called and told me to insert a Sengstaken–Blakemore tube, which was inserted through the mouth to manage upper gastrointestinal hemorrhage, usually a result of cirrhosis. The tube had been used since the 1950s. And while I had heard about the tube, I had never seen one, much less used one, so I was not comfortable with the prospect of inserting it into a critically ill patient. (The tube would eventually be replaced by modern endoscopic techniques that can rapidly and effectively control variceal bleeding, so Sengstaken–Blakemore tubes are rarely used anymore, at least in American hospitals.)

I told the attending that I was not familiar with the tube and asked if he wouldn't mind coming in to insert the tube. He told me I had no choice but to place the tube immediately because the patient was bleeding. He carefully explained over the phone how to do the procedure and said he was on his way in.

The Sengstaken–Blakemore device consists of a very large bore tube with two balloons at the end. After insertion the balloons are inflated with a blood pressure pump to compress the vessels in order to stop the bleeding. The trick is the tube has to be positioned correctly to work. Once the tube is inserted, the balloons are placed in proper position and inflated, the tube is kept in place with a two-pound (one kilogram) weight. To do that, a football helmet is placed on the head of the patient and the tube is attached to the helmet with the traction.

The patient was retching and vomiting blood all over the place. With the help of the nurses—who were great—I somehow managed to insert the tube, inflate the balloons, and attach the traction. But my relief was short-lived. Not long after the tube insertion, the patient died. When the attending arrived, he evaluated the situation then talked to the bereaved, crying family members. I sat in one corner of the nurses' station, drowned in all kinds of self-doubt and second-guessing. Facing the death of a patient, especially being in an unknown country with still unfamiliar surroundings, was difficult. I worried that I had placed the tube in his trachea instead of his stomach and caused his death. I was also apprehensive that the attending was going to be very angry with me and feared the repercussions from the patient's family.

The attending came out of the room and first talked to the nurses. When he approached me, I started to acknowledge that it was possible I did not place the tube in the right location. He stopped me mid-sentence and explained that the patient had lost too much blood to survive. He then thanked me for trying to help. The family members in turn also thanked me for trying to help their loved one. This gentle kindness offered to me by the family, during their time of anguish beyond measure, was an incredibly humbling experience.

The whole floor was sad, the patient's death leaving everyone wondering if there had been anything we could have done to save him. Eventually we accepted that it was not to be. Slowly things settled down, everyone picked up the pieces, and we went back to work knowing one death in the hospital could not stop us from preserving other lives.

It wasn't the first time I had seen a patient die; I saw many deaths while I was working in India. But the cirrhotic man's death was another example of how different it was to practice medicine in America. Even when a patient did not survive, at least the family knew everything that could be done to try and save their loved one had been done, using the best tools and knowledge currently available. Resources were not an issue. That was not always the case in India.

The medical school I attended was called the R. G. Kar Medical College and Hospital, which had a long, and proud history. Dr. Radha Gobindo Kar, popularly known as R. G. Kar, was an extraordinary person. He was admitted to a medical school in Calcutta. But he was very involved in Bengali dramas. Calcutta was the capital of culture, intellect, and arts in India and still is. He spent a lot of time playing in theaters all over Calcutta, neglecting his medical studies. It was one of the reasons that he went to Edinburgh to get his medical degree.

In 1886, Dr. Kar returned from Britain with the goal of establishing a medical school separate from the official institutions, which were then under British rule. He was bothered by the fact that the doctors at the Calcutta Medical College and Hospitals, run by the British government, were neglecting the local population. In 1886, Dr. Kar established the Calcutta Medical School, the first non-governmental medical college in Asia. At the invitation of Swami Vivekananda, an Irish lady named Margaret Elizabeth Nobel, later known as Sister Nivedita, came to Calcutta and helped Dr. Kar treat indigenous patients in the streets of Calcutta.

In 1916 the medical school merged with the College of Physicians and Surgeons of Bengal and was renamed Belgachia Medical College. The then governor of Bengal, Thomas Gibson-Carmichael, inaugurated the new incarnation, which welcomed forty-eight students. Starting from 1918 the college was called the Carmichael Medical College in honor of Lord Carmichael. In 1948, the name of the institution was permanently changed to the R. G. Kar Medical College and Hospitals. Dr. Kar wrote many books of medicine in the Bengali language for the convenience of the students and donated all his money to the school.

It was renowned for quality medical care, distinguished professors, and good medical education along with sports and cultural activities. Some of our students were members of the Indian Olympic soccer team. Students came from all over India as well as other parts of the world. The United States' National Institutes of Health's National Library of Medicine calls the college a medical pioneer. The maternity ward of my school was named after Sir Kedar Nath Das.

"In 1929 Sir Kedar Nath Das wrote the world-famous treatise on obstetric forceps. Another gynecologist, Dr. Subodh Mitra, was the pioneer of Mitra's operation for carcinoma cervix ... The noted cardiothoracic surgeon, Dr. Ajit Kumar Basu, achieved international fame for his work on noncirrhotic portal fibrosis. Prof. Subir Chatterjee, the noted pediatric surgeon, did the first surgery for esophageal atresia and separation of conjoined twins in India."

Dr. Mitra developed and pioneered an operation for cancer of the cervix which was known as Dr. Mitra's operation. He demonstrated his operation all over the world. The doctors in the United States mentioned Mitra's operation to me many times. When I attended school there, the hospital still provided free care, but the patients mostly had to buy their own medicines. We used to coax the medical representatives to give us some free medicine samples for the patients, and they usually did. I was in charge of the pediatric ward of the college hospital. Since our policy was to accept all admissions, we would have patients in beds, cribs, floors, and even on the verandas.

The patients were usually only babies and toddlers. Most came from rural areas, the parents carrying their babies to the hospital from miles away by open carts, by train, or in their arms as they walked. It could take days for them to reach the hospital, and they would arrive stressed, hungry, exhausted, and crying for help. Most of the time, it would be hours or days before they would reach the hospital, and most of the children arrived near death and unresponsive.

Tubercular meningitis was the primary affliction. The symptoms included high fever, rigid neck, vomiting, and diarrhea as well as convulsions because of swelling and pressure on the brain due to fluid buildup. The parents were dazed and often silent as a stark sadness enveloped them. Like everyone in the whole world, rich or poor, their sole wish was for their child to live.

These little patients were so weak they could barely whimper even when I performed a painful lumbar puncture using a needle to withdraw spinal fluid from their back to try and ease the pressure on the brain. For the procedure the patient was turned on their side. I would first scrub my hands with soap then rub them with alcohol. When I was ready the nurse would place the patient into an arched position by bringing the knees and head toward the chest, which increased the space between the vertebrae in the lower back. Using my fingers, I would locate the space where I could insert the syringe needle, which was about four inches long and very thin, then I would paint the skin with the mercurochrome as an antiseptic.

I needed the patient's body almost fixed, and the nurse would have to hold the patient very tightly so they could not move. That was extremely difficult because there was no local anesthesia. The procedure is painful, so the little ones would fight even though they were very sick. Their cries would often move the nurses to tears as I inserted the needle. It is a blind procedure because you had to do it by feel. That's why it was extremely critical for the patient to be still so I could feel the barely noticeable pop that indicated the needle had entered the space containing the spinal fluid. I would then withdraw the fluid into the syringe. You hoped to see just clear fluid. Cloudy or opaque fluid suggested an infection. You definitely did not want to see blood; that would mean a traumatic puncture, and the results would be unreliable.

I would send the collected spinal fluid to be cultured and stained for diagnosis. After doing many punctures I became expert at lumbar punctures and could successfully perform the procedure even on fighting kids. My professor would send me to do lumbar punctures on his private patients in their homes. I would carry the lumber puncture set with me. This enabled me to earn some extra money. Today the procedure is done much differently, with much less discomfort for the patients. And in the United States mercurochrome became illegal in 1998 because of its mercury content, replaced by safer antiseptics although it is still used in other parts of the world.

In some cases, the spinal canal would have no fluid because there was a blockage in the brain. I would then have to perform a cisterna puncture, which means placing a needle directly through the skull bones and brain into the cisterna, a space around the cerebellum where there is spinal fluid. The procedure would also reduce the pressure inside the brain, helping to prevent seizures. Again, there was no anesthesia involved, and our antiseptics were rudimentary. There was no ultrasound to direct the needles; it was another blind procedure. This procedure is done only in very sick and indicated patients.

But there were successes. Anita was five years old, with long, curly black hair and a pretty face. She had TB meningitis and was being treated at home in Calcutta by our Professor of Pediatrics, Dr. S. Dutta. She was not improving as expected and started to have some vision problems. Our professor thought Anita would need a spinal injection of streptomycin, a mainstay medicine for tuberculosis. When she was admitted to our ward, she had a low fever and was slightly sluggish but otherwise normal.

I had to give the spinal streptomycin daily. In the beginning she would cry, kick, and wiggle hard, trying to get out of the position. Her father would be there to calm and soothe her. After a few days she improved considerably. She started to bounce around, had a big infectious smile, and became a favorite patient of the nurses.

There was another patient who won everybody's heart. He was a patient of the ward. He suffered from cerebral palsy. He was there for many years, probably abandoned by his parents who were unable to take care of him. He could not sit up, stand, walk, or talk. He moved by rolling on the floor. He used to smile all the time and had bright eyes. The nurses used to dress him, feed him, and take care of him. It was like he was a family member.

Even though some of our patients did not get completely better or even survive, most of our patients improved and went home happy. Patients who stayed a little longer and bonded with the nurses usually got a farewell party and some sweets to take home. The families of the patients were always very grateful and that made us all very happy.

Finally, Anita was discharged home. I informally followed her progress at her home because of my friendship with her father. Ram Mitra was a very nice gentleman and very attentive to his daughter. He used to talk to me about her vision, which continued to deteriorate, although very slowly. Mr. Mitra worked in an iron foundry in Howrah, located across the Ganges from Calcutta, like Cambridge and Boston are across the Charles River from each other.

Later, as I was preparing to go to the States, I saw Mr. Mitra to say good-bye. He was sad and happy at the same time. I kept up correspondence with him. In one of his letters he informed me that his father had slight dementia. One evening, his father went out for a walk and never returned. Over time the letters trailed off and we lost touch.

Mr. Mitra was one of the lucky ones. Some parents and families who arrived crying, carrying a child would go home empty-handed despite our heroic efforts. But as doctors we became immune to that scenario. I vividly remember a tragic case where a four- or five-year-old boy was admitted with stridor, the high-pitched, wheezing sound caused by obstruction in the upper airways such as the voice box. It was a sign of severe respiratory distress, retracting his chest and neck muscles. His eyes were bulging as he tried desperately to take in one drop of air. He reached out to his parents, who stood helplessly at the foot of the bed, his skin turning blue and cold.

Even though I had started many IVs in these types of patients, I was having extreme difficulty. What this patient needed the most was a tracheostomy to create an airway, but reaching a surgeon by telephone was difficult. Instead we'd send an orderly with a note to the surgical ward for the surgeon on duty, requesting him to do the procedure. This messenger system took quite a bit of time because the wards were not next to each other. While waiting for the surgeon to arrive, my little patient was going downhill very fast, so in desperation I decided to do the procedure myself. But to our dismay, the child passed away just as the surgeon came. A horrible sadness overcame the parents and the rest of us.

About three years later, as a second-year surgical resident in the United States, I had to perform a bedside tracheostomy. One evening around eight o'clock, the operator paged me. Dr. Bernie was on the line and told me to do a tracheostomy on one of his patients. I told him the chief resident was on call, but he ordered me to do it in no uncertain terms. I was in a conundrum because I did not want to antagonize my ever-powerful chief resident, and at the same time I did not want to go against the attending. I decided to go ahead with the procedure and ran up to the seventh floor.

It was towards the end of the visiting hours, but some people were still milling around. I went with a nurse to see the patient, a twelve-year-old boy who was in extreme respiratory distress. He was fighting for air and retracting all his muscles. The boy's father was apprehensive and anxious and looked to me for answers. But I did not want to waste any valuable time, so I briefly explained his son's dire, life-and-death situation. The father begged me to do the best I could, and I assured him that I would.

I did not have much experience doing a bedside tracheostomy, but I thought if Dr. Bernie had chosen me over the chief resident, he must have seen something in me. The nurse and I gathered the tracheostomy tray with the necessary instruments and items including a knife, forceps, sutures, syringe, needle, Novocain, hook retractor, gauze, a tracheostomy tube, and many other things. It was a far cry from my experience in India. But it was still not optimal.

I asked the father to wait outside the room during the procedure.

We opened the tray on the bedside table. The gooseneck lamp served as the light source. We placed a small, rolled-up towel under the patient's back to extend his neck, the muscles moving and retracting. The nurse stood on the other side of the bed, making it difficult for her to reach across and help me. After everything was placed in order, the patient was moved into the proper position. We slid the lamp over to focus the light on the site of the procedure on the neck. After we gloved up I painted the skin with an antiseptic solution.

At each step we explained to the young patient what we were doing, but I wasn't sure he grasped it. I injected Novocain into the skin along the line of the incision then cut through the skin, the fatty layer underneath, and between the muscles. The trachea was exposed, but it was moving vigorously as he labored to breathe. I placed the hook retractor over a tracheal ring, a very important step, and instructed the nurse to hold it steady to prevent the trachea from moving. I made a small cut in it and removed a small piece of the tracheal cartilage to make a small hole. As soon as we accomplished that a blast of air came out through the opening, confirming that we were in the right place. There was absolutely no time to spare, and I inserted a metal tracheostomy tube with the obturator, which is inserted inside the tracheostomy tube to give it smoothness and to help ease the tube down the trachea. Once the tube was in place, I removed the obturator, and the young boy started to breathe normally, and all the muscles in his neck stopped retracting. He was calm and relaxed. I sutured the wound and fixed the tracheostomy tube with ties so that the tube would not come out.

While the nurse gathered the tray and instruments, I went to tell the boy's father the good news. He was overwhelmed with happiness and thanked me profusely. I then called Dr. Bernie, and he was also quite delighted with the outcome; he congratulated me for a good job.

Another morning I was making rounds with Dr. DeLeon, the chief of medicine. He was young, bright, knowledgeable, friendly, and a good educator. He was associated with Yale-New Haven Hospital. He was trying to place an IV in one of his patients. He was using a new device called an Intracath, a type of intravenous cannulation device in which a plastic catheter passes through a rigid needle and is inserted as a unit. When the vein is successfully entered the rigid needle is pulled back out of the vein, secured by tape to the skin as the needle cannot be removed, and the catheter is advanced into the vein. The plastic catheter remains inside the needle. (It is much different now and the needle is removable.) The upside of using this device was that the catheter could be kept in the vein for a longer period of time, reducing the number of times it needed to be changed, avoiding the painful punctures, as well as reducing the number of complications.

But the downside was that the sharp end of the needle would occasionally cut the intravenous catheter, which would disappear inside the vein, and retrieval was often difficult. That was exactly what happened when Dr. DeLeon was trying to insert the IV; the needle cut the catheter, and the catheter disappeared. That patient ended up being moved to Yale-New Haven Hospital. Fortunately, in 1973 the device was modified to eliminate this issue.

In a hospital you quickly learn to accept that not every outcome will end well, and you find satisfaction and appreciation in those that do. Even though the patients I treated at Griffin hospital were not babies or children from far away towns as I often encountered in India, it was still sad when someone passed.

On one hand deaths in the American hospital were so very different from what I had experienced in medical school. There was no hunger, no exhaustion, no desperation among the patients. Americans as a whole are much more knowledgeable about medical conditions and health matters. The hospital surroundings were much nicer. Everything was delightful on the floor, except for the death. But even then that scenario was much less cruel than how we experienced death in India.

On the other hand, death is always cruel regardless of geography.

So This is America

Compared to summers in Calcutta, the weather in Connecticut was very pleasant and enjoyable. I'd often go for walks with some of my compatriots from India, and sometimes the people we'd pass would stop us and make conversation. They would ask where we came from, as there were not many Indians around. Some told us about their experience in India while posted there during World War II. They would usually say it was a beautiful country and they liked the people there. They also appreciated us helping their country during the war.

I was getting used to the hospital and medical system, and as days rolled by I felt increasingly comfortable with the daily routine. It was getting easier to speak English, and I became friendly with many hospital personnel. We'd sit at the nurse's stations, talking and joking.

One day a nurse's aide named Mrs. Gargano invited some of us to go ocean fishing on her husband's boat. None of us had ever been out on the ocean. It would be a novel experience, so we jumped at the idea. Going out on a boat to do some deep-sea fishing, maybe catching fish and having our lunch, could not get any better. I was equally excited and apprehensive. Living in India the Atlantic Ocean seemed so, so far away and only known through our geography book. I wondered how risky the excursion was going to be. I couldn't wait to go fishing then write about it to my family; they would be surprised beyond belief.

At that point I had only ever been to an ocean beach once, not long after I first arrived. On my way to the hospital one day I bumped into Jack and Jill, interns from England who lived off campus. I was very surprised to see that both their faces were lobster red, slightly swollen, and had small, broken blisters. I asked what had happened to them.

With a little smirk, Jack said, "The weather was good, so we went to the beach to enjoy our off day. We both fell asleep on the sand and got sunburned."

Then he suggested that I should go to the beach. While the sunburn was not exactly a selling point, Jack incited a little curiosity in me about going to the beach. I had seen some pictures of ocean beaches but had never been to one. I asked Samar if he was interested in going to the beach because I knew he liked the water and was also interested in doing new, different things. Samar immediately agreed, and we decided to go to a nearby beach. Not having any clue about the beaches in the United States, we went there fully dressed, wearing long-sleeved shirts, trousers, dress socks, and regular shoes. Obviously, we were like fish out of water.

We approached the beach and saw many women lying on the sand under the sun in small bathing suits. It was so odd to us. We wondered how they could be so exposed in front of everybody. Remember, we had just arrived in this country and extreme modesty is part of our native culture. There were also men in their swimming trunks sunbathing, and little kids were playing in the sand with their shovels and buckets. The water was full of people swimming, riding the waves, or just standing around. Boats were visible sailing in the distance.

We were a little flummoxed and apprehensive.

I said to Samar, "I don't know if we should be here."

He shrugged.

I said, "To go down to the beach we would have to walk between almost-naked ladies; would it be proper?"

"Listen," Samar said. "We came all the way to the beach; we're going down there."

We took our shoes and socks off, rolled our pants up, and sauntered through the sand then into the ocean. The water was a little cool, waves were not too big, and under the beautiful, blue sky, it was rather pleasant. However, I was very self-conscious, convinced people were looking at us wondering: *Who are these guys walking around fully clothed on the beach?*

After absorbing the nuances of the beach and feeling desperately out of place, we slowly made out way back up. Even though it had been a bit uncomfortable, we enjoyed our short excursion. And the best part was we did not fall asleep on the beach and get sunburned. I felt much less apprehensive about our planned fishing trip and looked forward to being back at the ocean.

Mrs. Gargano told us that she would pick us up in the

morning and drive us down to the boat, where we'd meet her husband. On the day of our excursion, Mrs. Gargano arrived in a beautiful, red convertible.

She said, "Boys, are you ready for the boat ride and fishing?"

She always called us boys; we did not mind and did not know the difference. But I never felt it was meant in any kind of derogatory way; from Mrs. Gargano it was a sign of affection.

We all climbed into the car; I'd never been in a convertible before. Driving down the road as she sped up and the air started blowing into our faces and tousling our hair was also a brand-new and exciting experience.

We were riding through beautiful neighborhoods with tree-lined roads fronting well-tended and well-kept houses that were all very similar to each other. Cookie-cutter homes. Back in India there was no uniformity, with each house looking unique. But even with a lack of individuality, the scenery was very picturesque. Young men were washing and waxing their cars, and I imagined it was probably for a date later that night. Many people, some in shorts, were watering or mowing their lawns.

Where I grew up the average homeowner did not have lawns—manicured or otherwise. However, India is a diverse country, and there were many rich people with massive mansions boasting sculpted lawns. They would employ workers who would cut the grass by hand using large scissors. Or the workers might use a drum-like mower drawn by an ox. For those who were not wealthy but did have a lawn, mowing was not an issue because their goats and cows would graze on it, keeping the grass shorn.

Many years after that day, I saw a pediatrician colleague

of mine mowing his lawn as I was driving by his house. I pulled over and told him that he should buy some goats who would keep the grass trimmed by grazing on it, and we had a little laugh about it. But then not that long ago I was playing golf and discovered that the maintenance people at the course were using goats to keep the poison ivy in check. And I have since read that some homeowners with a lot of land were using goats instead of a mower to be more environmentally conscious. Funny how cultures repurpose customs from one another.

As I was riding in the convertible and enjoying the scenery, I daydreamed a little about how when I went back home to Calcutta after finishing my training in the States, I would build a house like the ones we were passing, and I would put in a lawn and a flower garden. I wondered when that day would come.

After our scenic ride we arrived at the pier. Mrs. Gargano introduced us to her husband, Thomas, and after a round of greetings, we walked down to the dock. There were many boats of different sizes and colors with their names painted on, like *Daisy* and *Molly*, written in different elegant fonts. Our boat was named *Super Fast*. Thomas told us how much he loved his boat but didn't have the time to go out on it as much as he would like.

Before boarding we put on life jackets while Tom was untying the ropes anchoring *Super Fast* to the pier. Once we were all seated, Tom started the engine and navigated *Super Fast* out into the open water. By then it was just after midday, and even though it was windy, the sun was scorching hot even for us Indians. But the water was a beautiful blue, and the silvery waves were dancing under the glittering sun. After a short ride we reached the fishing spot, and

Tom took out the gear, handing me a fishing rod with a lure. He then instructed us how to throw the line. It was difficult because the boat was rocking quite a bit, and we had to hold on to something to keep standing, but somehow we managed to get our lines in the water.

Then the fun began. The boat was not small, but it was getting vigorously tossed back and forth as the wind-driven waves crashed against the hull. A few of my friends got seasick and threw up. I was doing alright physically but was very nervous because it felt like we could capsize if a big enough wave hit us. Even though I was hoping we would go back to the dock, I didn't want to let on just how worried and fearful I was. Tom had intended to go even further out to sea but in light of the wind—and the seasickness—he felt the water was too rough and cut our excursion short. I was so relieved at his decision to head back in. At the same time a part of me was also a little disappointed that we couldn't be more adventurous. But I trusted Tom's judgment to not put us at risk.

When we got back on dry land, Mrs. Gargano drove us back to her house. Coming in from the heat, her air-conditioned house seemed freezing. Tom offered us beer—I believe it was a Schlitz—and being very thirsty I accepted. I didn't like it and only drank half the can. I got a headache, probably a combination of the beer and an empty stomach. Mrs. Gargano made me a sandwich, which helped my headache.

While eating I shared my limited experience with drinking. When I was in medical school, a junior classmate of mine took me to a bar in Calcutta. He was Christian and came from South India, so I presumed he was used to drinking; there is nothing in Hindu doctrine that prohibits alcohol. It was more that those in my socioeconomic class generally did not indulge in alcohol, and it was out of the question in my family. Broadly speaking the Indians most likely to drink are those in the labor class or those in the higher socioeconomic class, the latter likely to have been exposed to Western culture by going abroad or having more British ties in India.

The bar my friend took me to was very busy. He ordered beer for both of us. After taking a few sips, I excused myself and went to the bathroom. I felt dizzy and wobbly, but it was likely psychological and not physiological. When I rejoined my friend, I mostly pretended to sip my beer because I found it difficult to drink. I was saved from having to try and finish it because my friend suggested we go to a different bar.

The new locale was more than just a watering hole; it was what I now know is an exotic dance club. There were scantily dressed girls dancing on a stage, and the tables around the stage were crammed full of men who were drinking and calling out to the young women. There was so much male energy I was worried a fight might break out. I was quite naïve and could not believe such a place existed in Calcutta. While my friend was enjoying his life without the leash of his family's restrictions, I did not feel comfortable at all. In fact, I felt guilty and was glad that we left the bar soon after.

But at Mrs. Gargano's we sat around comfortable sofas as we ate our sandwiches and sipped our drinks. This time I did not feel as guilty for drinking beer, perhaps because now I was the one unleashed from my family's expectations, like my friend in Calcutta. Conversation flowed easily with Mrs. Gargano and Tom and mostly centered on how different lifestyles were between India and the

United States. It was a relaxing respite from working at the hospital.

We visited for so long I was worried we might be overstaying our welcome and suggested it was time to go. They drove us back to the hospital and after thanking them again for the very interesting afternoon, said our good-byes. As we walked to our rooms, we all agreed how nice they were to have taken so much trouble for our enjoyment. Such kindnesses and thoughtfulness made me feel more welcome and at home in what was still a strange, new land.

That was summer, and she had some surprises for the winter. She was a skater and asked if we would be interested in ice skating. I had seen skating while lounging in the TV room. I thought that was a novel idea and wanted to try that out. One night she took a couple of us to her club. The club house was a small log cabin on a frozen pond. Inside there were skates on the racks and a stereo system attached to a loudspeaker outside. There was a bright floodlight illuminating the pond.

Mrs. Gargano helped us to put the skates on. I had absolutely no idea what it was going to be like. We put on some of the hats and gloves that were on the racks, which did not fit very well. We probably looked like clowns. Fortunately, nobody else was there. She helped us to stand up on the skates and have some basic instructions. The big light was on and the music was playing. She took us one at a time onto the ice and skated by holding us. She then went skating by herself, turning, speeding with the outstretched arms, and enjoying herself. What happened to us? We tried to stand and kept falling. We probably did it a thousand times and finally she took us in. We were glad to get warm. Mrs. Gargano said it would take a little practice before we could skate. It was not a peasant experience, and I never tried it again.

Between getting settled in and work, it was a while before I got a haircut since coming to the United States. I came to find out that there was a barbershop within walking distance of the hospital. Even though a haircut was a small matter, I was still a little nervous.

Back in India, the barber used to come to the house to give us a haircut, particularly when we were young. We would sit on a couple of stacked up bricks out in the open. My father used to supervise the haircut. The barber carried his scissors, a manual clipper, a small mirror, a brush, soap, and a small bowl for water in a six-by-eight-inch wooden box, which also contained a folding straight razor for shaving. The barber used a narrow razor for cutting toenails and fingernails, which was included with the haircut.

For a drape the barber would make a hole in an unfolded newspaper, slip it over our head, and start cutting our hair. If my father did not like some part of the haircut, he would ask the barber to fix it. The barber usually obliged. We could not enter the house after a haircut until we showered, which for us was a bucket shower using well water.

When I was older, barbers with their boxes would come to the medical school dorm and give students a haircut the same way, except we sat on chairs instead of bricks. Most everybody showered before entering their rooms there too.

Occasionally I would go to a barbershop, variously called a barber saloon or hair cutting saloon—not a salon. You'd sit in one of the wooden chairs placed in front of mirrors. There the barber used a piece of cloth to cover your body instead of newspaper, but the tools were the same. On request they would cut your nails and also give a shave.

I warily entered the barbershop for my first American haircut. It was brightly lit, with large mirrors encircled with lights and no bulbs hanging from the ceiling. I was surprised to see that the barbers were wearing the same uniform we wore at the hospital: white pants and white shirts with the buttons on the left shoulder.

I sat down in a chair that was not only comfortable but could also go up and down and rotate 360 degrees—a far cry from the wooden chairs in India. There was a board in front listing the prices for the various services. I never knew that you could get a shampoo in a barbershop, for $2. I felt that the barbers were Italians because mine greeted me with: *Hey, paisan*, which I had heard many Italians in the hospital say.

"Are you from Sicily?" he asked.

Many Italians took me for a Sicilian. "No, I am from India."

We talked about politics, sports, movies, and many other topics. It seems to me that barbershops all over the world are a place for public discourse and social interaction. We did the same thing back home. Some things never change! In Bengali we call this enjoyable conversation an *adda*.

My apprehension was long gone; getting an American haircut was a pleasant experience.

Hospital life rolled on. Work became easier and somewhat routine. As the initial newness and excitement wore off, staying around the hospital on my nights and weekends off was becoming somewhat boring. There wasn't a lot to do. We had a black-and-white TV in our lounge—this was before color TVs became readily available—and I tried watching the evening news but had a hard time understanding the newscasters. It was odd that I could understand people speaking English when talking to them face-to-face but not when watching TV, so I could not enjoy any of the series, talk shows, or movies broadcast on TV.

Sports was a different problem. American football, baseball, basketball, and golf were very unfamiliar. And I found no channel that aired soccer or cricket games. But I eventually found two TV shows I enjoyed. One was *Hootenanny*, a musical variety show that aired from a different college campus each week, featuring popular groups of the period. I liked the songs and the young students, some seemingly in love, who gathered around and swayed to the music.

I always liked music. Bengali pop music was my favorite while growing up. I did not care too much about Indian classical music. After coming to the States, I was exposed to Western culture and music, mainly American pop. I was somewhat familiar with rock 'n roll. Some of my upstart classmates used to sing those songs. Some of the songs that caught my ear were "Big Girls Don't Cry," "Walk Right In," and songs performed by bands like the Kingston Trio. I started to enjoy the rhythm, the beats, the tunes, and the singers.

One Sunday morning Jiten and I were going somewhere. It was a nice sunny day with beautiful bright white snow lining the sidewalks. I saw well-dressed people with children coming out of a church after a mass. I liked the snapshot of that scene. As we kept driving a beautiful tune was playing on the radio that stayed with me. I found out later it was called "Greensleeves."

For some unknown reason I started appreciating Indian classical music, particularly sitar. Ravi Shankar was giving concerts all over the world, including the States. Just before I came here, Shankar composed music for the award-winning movie *Pather Panchali* (*The Ballads of Life*), which was directed by Satyajit Ray (the first Indian filmmaker to get an honorary Academy Award for Lifetime Achievement). I continue to enjoy all kinds of music, including pop music and the classical music of Beethoven, Mozart, and Chopin, to name a few.

I started watching boxing; there was not much to understand. I used to watch the Friday night fights sponsored by Gillette, and if I remember correctly, a fluttering butterfly opened the show.

I became somewhat friendly with Mr. Shea, who worked in the accounts department and also liked boxing. One night he invited me to go with him to watch a replay of the third Ingemar Johansson–Floyd Patterson fight. The first fight had taken place in June 1959 at Yankee Stadium. Johansson was the undefeated European champion, and Patterson had lost only one professional fight. Patterson was favored to win, so it was quite the upset when Johansson won.

Their rematch took place a year later at New York's Polo Grounds, and Patterson became the first heavyweight champion to regain his title by knocking Johansson out. The third and final was March 1961 in Miami Beach. Patterson won by a sixth-round knockout. I still remember Johansson lying flat on his back with quivering legs. It was quite exciting for me not only because this was the first boxing match I saw on TV in my entire life, but also because it was a knockout. Those two losses to the American were the only ones in Johansson's professional career, and he retired in 1963 with a 28-2 record.

Watching that final bout was exciting, even though I knew how it ended, and overall the evening with Mr. Shea, away from the hospital, was very pleasant. And watching a great fight resulted in me getting hooked on boxing, still one of my favorite sports. Characters such as the flamboyant Jack Johnson, the greatest ever Cassius Clay/Muhammed Ali, colorful commentator Howard Cosell, boxing corner doctor and writer Freddie Pacheco, and many others gave me much pleasure and entertainment in those early years of my career in the United States.

Homesick

I eventually moved into the surgery rotation and quickly learned that the operating room supervisor—an experienced nurse—controls the operating room. She was the conductor of the OR symphony.

There were some irascible surgeons in our hospital, like the urologist who always managed to lose his scrubs in the middle of a surgery, no matter how many times the supervisor reprimanded him. Since he was scrubbed, the nurses would have to tie him up again. Another doctor—who was not a very good surgeon—would always arrive late and start yelling at everybody.

One day he gave me the scalpel to do an appendectomy. I was horrified. Even though I'd seen appendectomies while in medical school, I was just beginning my rotation, so I had no hands-on surgical experience. No matter; apparently there was no dry run, no assisting first. I made the incision according to his instruction but then could not proceed further. Even though he was trying to help me to learn the procedure, it was too early in the game for me to take the lead. Thankfully, he took over and finished the surgery. The typical process is to learn surgery in baby steps, with the surgeon present through the entire case. But I didn't blame him for putting me in that position; I don't think he realized my absolute inexperience.

One day I was making rounds with the chief of surgery, Dr. DuPage. He was short in stature, with a balding head and always sharply dressed. He was a moderately good surgeon, a nice fellow, and didn't bother us too much. As we were walking between the beds, we could hear the piped-in music overhead. Dr. DuPage stopped, told me to listen to the piano playing in the song, and commented on its beauty. I was not familiar with Western music, so I did not recognize the melody or the singer. He started to hum along and explained it was Tony Bennett, which of course did not mean a thing to me, but I nodded politely. A few years later, after becoming more familiar with American music and culture, I realized the song we'd listened to was "I Left My Heart in San Francisco." By then I could appreciate how beautiful the melody and lyrics were and are, and how the song isn't just about the city by the Bay. It's about wistfulness for wherever you come from, about nostalgia for days gone by, about a part of you always remaining from whence you came. And now I can never hear the song without thinking of India—and Dr. DuPage.

My rotation in the emergency room was during the summer, so it was common to have worried and anxious patients coming in to have us inspect mosquito and similar insect bites. If they thought a little red bump was bad … in India we had to worry about scorpions' stings, which could prove fatal to small children. We also were plagued with malaria. But in the United States malaria was officially eradicated in 1951, and Lyme disease wasn't identified yet, so when I was an intern, mosquito and other bug bites were nothing more than an itchy nuisance.

One of the first steps for differentiating between a minor and serious bug bite or sting is to work through some of the key symptoms. Significant pain, swelling, and bruising are all signs that a bite may be serious. Swelling that is spreading significantly beyond the initial bite may also be a sign of a serious issue. So only in extreme instances will a bug bite reaction be grave enough to warrant an ER visit. During my time in Connecticut, I came across very few life-threatening events, so it was very perplexing to me and the other Indian house officers to see people complain about harmless bites, and it became a private joke among us.

Soon summer was ending. I could feel a chill in the air at night, and the leaves started to change. Crimson, red, yellow, and orange—it was a celebration of colors so beautiful to see and enjoy. As they fell to the ground, the variegated colors of the leaves made artistic patterns. We called it autumn in India, but many in Connecticut referred to it as fall, a new term. And a fitting one as the leaves fell off the trees and were strewn from city streets and suburban lawns to pastures and fields.

The hospital was in a small town where it seemed everyone was an enthusiastic football fan—American football I should say. To India and the rest of the world, football is soccer. Everyone from the doctors and nurses to the hospital personnel encouraged us to go to see the local high school games. Since none of us had a car, we walked down to the field. There was a band of school students playing trumpets, saxophones, and drums, creating a festive atmosphere. I was surprised to see that there was a small stadium with stands for spectators to sit; our schools and colleges in India did not have stadiums of their own. But we were a little shy, so we stood on one side of the field to watch American football. Our first impressions were the same: what a vicious game, but it was also exciting and a nice distraction from our daily routine.

One October night some of us were outside, sitting on a hill near our quarters, shooting the breeze beneath a beautiful, bright, and clear blue sky. As I stared up at the glittering stars in between wisps of white clouds illuminated by the moon, I suddenly remembered this was Durga Puja time back home.

Durga Puja is a Hindu celebration of the warrior goddess Durga, and her defeat of the evil buffalo demon, Mahishasura. It's probably the biggest five-day festival in the world. It's more than just a religious holiday; Puja also celebrates culture. It starts with elaborately crafted statues of Durga put up on display throughout the town, similar to how people decorate and display Christmas trees. At the end of the festival, the statues are paraded through the streets, accompanied by music and dancing.

My siblings and I grew up with the goddess Durga, and as little kids, we'd visit the sculptors almost every day to watch them bring the goddess to life. They would first build a bamboo frame, shape it with hay, then apply a special clay to create the figure of the goddess's body. The sculpted figures were usually at least ten feet tall and equally wide.

Durga is depicted with ten arms, her children on her side, and riding a lion while spearing the devil to get rid of all the evils in the world. The clay figure would be painted in bright colors, dressed in a silk sari, and decorated with many imitation jewels. When finished a veil would cover her face, and the statue would be kept hidden behind a curtain. Finally, on a particularly auspicious night determined by astronomers, she would be given life by the priest, and the veil would be removed. Once everybody could see her, the entire town would light up.

Again, like Christmas, people would go puja shopping, and everybody would get new clothes for each day of the festival. Women would wear new gold jewelry and nice-smelling perfumes. We couldn't afford to buy clothes at stores, so my father would buy the fabric, and my sister Nadi would measure us, design the outfits, cut the fabric, then spend all night sewing. We always got compliments from people admiring her work.

Families, groups of friends, and children would go out at night and visit all the pandals, which are theme-based, temporary structures representing the goddess's house that displays a Durga statue. Pandals are typically elaborately decorated, and there can be literally hundreds of them located throughout town, so we tried to visit as many as possible each night. Many people would leave food or flowers for the goddess.

A month or so before the puja, we would wake up very early in the morning to a floating sound of the drummers practicing for the puja—it remains a very nostalgic memory even now. During the puja there are many traditions. In one a priest adds mustard oil to some brass pots, puts in a cotton wick, and lights it. He then attaches the flaming pots to a handle so he can carry it as he dances to accompanying music, such as bells and drums, while also chanting mantras, facing the image of the goddess. The drummers will be playing the drums and young people would dance with smoking clay pots in their hands. As kids we loved to set off fireworks. Crowds would flock to see the goddesses, the pandals, the lighting, and the decorations. These enchanting evenings would go on for five nights.

At the end of the festival, people would gather in the pandal and smear abir on each other and on the goddess after the priests chanted a good-bye mantra. The statues of the goddesses were transported to a nearby river on trucks with much fanfare as crowds of people line the streets to see all the goddess statues going by. Others follow behind the vehicles all the way to the river, where special steps are set up leading into the water. With music playing and fireworks exploding, the goddesses are immersed in the water and float away.

In my hometown of Jalpaiguri, the immersion was more spectacular. People would hire boats that were almost like barges, which would be joined together side-by-side. The large image of the Durga would be placed on a platform placed in the middle of the connected boats. While the drummers played, the priest chanted, and fireworks lit the night sky, the boats would circle seven times in the river while we watched from the shore, enjoying the beauty of the goddesses until they were put in the water and disappeared beneath the water. Durga goes back to her inlaws, thus signifying Durga's return to her home.

After the immersion we'd return home feeling sad. The end of Durga puja always brought an emotional letdown because there was so much anticipation before it arrived and then it consumed us for five days. After returning home, we would touch the feet of our elders as a sign of respect, what we call *Pranam*. It is also a tradition to visit friends and relatives, wish them well, and offering customary sweets in the days following immersion.

Growing up in India we never gave a second thought to disposing of the statues in our rivers and lakes. But in another case of traditional customs butting heads with modern practicality, the hundreds of thousands of statues dumped every year has become a major pollution problem. Specifically, some of the materials used to make the statues disintegrate and pollute the water.

Local governments are trying to encourage the statue builders to use materials that will dissolve quickly and sink to the river or lake floor, and natural food coloring instead of any chemical-based paint. Some municipalities are also pushing to have dedicated immersion pools built that can be used at the end of the festival instead of natural bodies of water. Somehow, that just won't have the same emotional impact, the same cultural ties going back centuries. It won't create the same indelible memories that were so vivid that October night in Connecticut, when the pristine sky, the clouds, and the chill in the air reminded me of so many nights spent rejoicing during puja.

Recalling all the good times we'd shared during the festivals brought a stab of homesickness. I was missing my family, and I knew they were missing me. This was the first time my family and I weren't together during the puja. And the friends I was talking to were from different parts of India and did not share the same sentiments I did. Thinking about the joy and fun they were experiencing at the puja while I was so far away made me sad.

It was getting late, and we were all tired, so we called it a night and went back to our respective rooms. I fell asleep with a homesick, lonely heart. But when I woke up, it was a new day and a new chance to continue learning about medicine, and the thoughts of puja slipped away.

Talking Turkey

The days were getting darker earlier and the nights were getting much colder, requiring more covers in bed. The trees were mostly bare now and looked as if they were standing around without any clothes, their once-colorful leaves now blanketing the ground in brown clumps. Everybody in the hospital was talking turkey—literally. The Thanksgiving holiday was approaching, and it seemed as if everyone's thoughts were consumed with the anticipation of eating turkey.

My co-workers asked if we had turkeys in India; to answer meant I had to figure out what exactly a turkey was. A little research later and I understood my ignorance. Turkeys are native to North America; while there are breeds of turkey raised now in India, my town was turkey-free.

But now everywhere I looked I was surrounded by turkeys. There were paper cutouts of turkeys wearing old-fashioned hats hung in the hospital lobby. Magazine covers had pictures of succulent looking cooked turkeys. People talked excitedly about Turkey Day. It was apparently a national American obsession.

I was somewhat embarrassed that I didn't understand what Thanksgiving was about. The way people talked, it sounded like a holiday set aside for eating turkeys and watching American football. Again, a little research educated me on the early European settlers and them celebrating their first harvests. India had many such festivals dating back probably thousands of years; that I could relate to. Dr. Richard Feldman, one of the hospital's pediatricians, invited me to Thanksgiving turkey dinner at his house. I was very excited. I couldn't wait to taste this gorgeous turkey meat that people were so drooling over.

Thanksgiving arrived on a chilly but beautifully sunny and clear day. Dr. Feldman picked me up from the hospital, and we drove to his large home that boasted manicured lawns in the front and back. Inside he had a houseful including relatives, friends, and associates I recognized from the hospital. Some were drinking wine or beer. I was offered a drink but declined, remembering my past adverse reactions to beer.

It was exciting to see so many people engaged in different conversations, and I soon joined into some conversations and got comfortable in the surroundings. When it was time to carve the turkey, Dr. Feldman called me over and proudly presented the cooked bird for my auspicious inaugural sighting. To me it just looked like the world's biggest chicken, but I responded with suitable appreciation.

The carving was done with great fanfare and a very large knife. The carver really loved the looks of the meat, its color, the smell, and said it was gorgeous. The house remained full of conversation and chatter, and I was enjoying being part of the day's celebration.

People were asking me if we ate turkey in India. They were really curious about the kinds of food we eat, how the food was cooked. Did we cook on an electric or gas stove? Did we use knives and forks? Did we refrigerate food? Some of them experienced Indian food in restaurants and liked it. I tried to describe our ancient methods.

While most Americans probably primarily think of curry when talking about Indian food, Indian cuisine can vary greatly from one region to the next. In Bengal, there is an emphasis on fish—especially fresh sweet water varieties—vegetables, lentils, and rice. While Indian restaurants in the United States can have good food, it is not anything like the food that I grew up eating. And certainly our cooking circumstances and eating traditions are very different.

For example, since we had no electricity, we cooked using a portable clay oven that used coal. To light the coal we would gather sticks and other combustibles around our house. But mostly we used cow dung, which I now find a bit embarrassing. But you would see people with buckets following cows around, waiting to collect the dung. It started as a matter of necessity because wood is often scarce. The dung would be shaped into circular patties called *ghute* and dried. It was very helpful during monsoon time as the stored ghutes would stay dry, and the gathered kindling would be wet and difficult to light. And since we always had the windows and doors open, we weren't in danger of the coal's harmful gasses as it burned.

At home dinner was eaten in shifts. First the children would eat. After washing our hands we'd sit on the kitchen floor, sometimes on wooden squares that were only a few inches high. Everyone had their own brass plates called *thala* with rice in it. The other food items such as dal, vegetable curry, and fish curry would be placed in individual small bowls or be served one item at a time. Egg curry was a treat, as was *luchi*, a puffed bread made from special flour that is usually eaten with fried eggplant or a special potato curry, *aloor dum*, that is scrumptious. We would infrequently have eggs as they were expensive. One boiled egg would be divided into thin slices using a sewing thread, curried, and then each person would get one slice. By tradition and culture, we only used our right hands when eating.

We were taught to eat at a moderate pace; eating too quickly is considered rude, and eating too slowly might be construed as you disliking the food. Once the kids finished the adult men would eat. When they had finished, the adult women would have their dinner. The last person to eat was our mom, once she served everyone else.

Classes at my school in Jalpaiguri started at 10:30 a.m. and ended at 4:00 p.m. Almost every day after a breakfast of flatbread with some molasses or puffed or flattened rice with milk, one of us brothers would go to the open-air bazaar to buy vegetables and fish. Vendors came from distant villages carrying their produce in multiple baskets on their heads. They would sit down on the ground, display their goods such as potatoes, eggplants, pumpkins, okra, mangoes, and jackfruits. Many different kinds of fish were sold—some still alive. We ate only freshwater fish from the rivers, no sea fish. My mother started cooking as soon as the food was brought back from the market.

Our staples were rice and lentils, vegetables, and fish curry. Basmati rice was used only on special occasions such as weddings and religious festivities. We were very fond of boiled and fried vegetables. We'd mix boiled potatoes with mustard oil, chili pepper, and onion. Since there was no refrigeration, meals always had to be cooked from scratch.

There were usually no snacks in-between meals except for afternoon tea. We were not allowed to drink tea until we went to college.

The food in Indian restaurants in the United States is very different from what I grew up with. It is not only very different from the Bengali dishes, but it is not traditional daily food anywhere in India. They asked me many questions and were surprised to learn the significant differences.

We all sat down at a long dinner table with expensive-looking plates and an assortment of cutlery—another novel experience. In contrast, in India on festive occasions the food might be presented on banana leaves placed before the guests, who'd sit on the floor. Banana leaves are still used occasionally even if the guests are sitting at the table.

We selected portions of the meat and other foods as the serving trays were passed from person to person. The people sitting around me urged me to try the white meat of the turkey, which I did. Most of the dishes were unfamiliar to me so I ended up with a piece of turkey breast, one large skinned boiled potato, what I learned later was cranberry sauce, and a little lettuce.

By then I was familiar with the etiquette of the napkin, and the use of forks and knives was also easier. But I was waiting for the others to start eating so that I could follow their lead. Finally, I cut into the turkey meat. People up and down the table were going gaga over it, complementing Dr. Feldman on how moist and tasty it was.

Anticipating culinary nirvana, I took a bite of the white turkey meat in my mouth and nearly choked. The meat was so bland, so tasteless, and devoid of any spices that my taste buds became unconscious. If I could have spit it out, I would have. I could barely swallow it but forced myself to eat that piece and a couple more.

Now what to do with the bald, burly potato sitting in one corner of my plate? I was perplexed. Ordinarily I would mash the potato, which was smaller than the brute on my plate here, mix it with mustard oil, onion, and chili peppers—delicious. But there was no mustard oil or chili pepper. I cut the potato following the action of the person sitting next to me. They put sour cream and butter on the potato, but I was not adventurous enough to try that concoction. So that lonely potato would not be devoured by me. While the cranberry sauce tasted good, my plate was heaped up with the food that I would not eat. It was embarrassing. And nobody suggested I cover the food with gravy, nor did I know that was a most popular food.

I managed to disguise my lack of appetite by covering the meat and potato beneath excess lettuce and tomato. People were eagerly waiting for my review of the meal. I twisted the truth. I said that the turkey was delicious and everything else was scrumptious. I was offered a second helping of everything but politely declined.

After the dessert—now that was truly delicious—and

coffee, we relocated to the living room. The conversation turned to the differences between Indian and American culture such as language (there are twenty-three official languages identified in the Indian constitution; one in the United States); food (refer to Thanksgiving meal review), and transportation (India is the land of trains; Americans have a love affair with cars).

I realized that much of what Americans think they know about India came from movies. One of the doctors gave me a scenario: If while waiting for a train, a girl dropped a magazine on the platform and I picked it up and gave it back to her, would that start a dating relationship? I told him that only happened in (cheesy) movies. Then I had to explain that there was no dating in India because most marriages were still arranged. Which is not the same as forced. In many ways a marriage was a relationship between families and not so much a relationship between just two people. American culture, which was still less than two hundred years old, was in its infancy when compared to a country like India. And it had been forged, defined, and informed by its fight for independence and belief that the entire continent was its oyster. Personal freedom and happiness were in the American DNA. Not so much in India, where family traditionally took precedence over the individual. Even well into the twenty-first century, that would still generally be true.

Even though the potato and the turkey did not agree with me, I must say that I enjoyed my Thanksgiving excursion very much; the congregation of people and the festive atmosphere reminded me of home. When Dr. Feldman dropped me back at the hospital, I sincerely thanked him for giving me the opportunity to experience a slice of American life, and for their cordiality, hospitality, and kindness.

The next day at work, several people asked if I had enjoyed my first Thanksgiving turkey. I just smiled and said it was truly indescribable, and they walked away pleased. A white lie of misdirection, I suppose, but one I was happy to live with.

Rides and Rotation

Looking for any chance to spend time away from the hospital, I agreed to sign up for an international students day after one of the hospital volunteers urged me to. Even though I wasn't technically a student, the foreign interns were allowed to participate, and I was assigned a host family to spend the weekend with. My host was Mr. Foley, who worked at a local tire factory as a chemist. I would spend a night at the Foley house, and we would do various activities together over the weekend.

Mr. Foley and his young son picked me up at the hospital, and the ride to his house was picturesque and surprisingly bucolic. We passed by many wide-open pastures dotted with horses and grazing cows, followed by stretches thick with trees that seemed to glow against brilliant blue sky. I was almost disappointed when we reached his home because it meant the drive was over.

Like the other American homes I'd been to, the Foley family had a nice house. He introduced me to his wife, Mary, who was warm and welcoming. We sat down for a small tea break before heading to a planned international student gathering, which was held in a large hall. There were finger foods and cold drinks provided, a nice touch.

The participants, who came from Europe, Japan, Africa, Latin America, and elsewhere, included students, researchers, some professionals on sabbatical, and other interns like me. What we all had in common was our youth and that we were starting our lives with unfettered aspirations. Everybody was impeccably dressed, wearing traditional clothing of gorgeous colors with exquisite patterns depicting individual countries' traditions. We talked about all kinds of things—from politics to education to sports—and were intensely interested in each other. Even though not everybody spoke English well, that was no problem for carrying on a conversation. I was sad when that amazingly interesting evening wound down.

I had always been interested in meeting people from different countries and cultures. I even had pen pals in Europe, including one in Scandinavia whose father was a doctor. He once sent me a picture of the midnight sun. Unfortunately, the postage for mailing letters became too expensive for me, and I had to stop corresponding. So, having the chance to talk to people from around the world face-to-face was extraordinary, and more than compensated for the loss of my pen pal. I said good-bye to my newfound friends and hoped we would meet again. I must mention that my father once said to me that I would not need pen pals if I succeed in life; I would meet people from other countries. He was so correct.

It was still early evening when we got back to Mr. Foley's house, so we sat in the living room, had a cup of tea, and discussed politics—specifically Indian politics. Whereas the United States has traditionally only had two major parties at a time, India has a multi-party system that recognizes national, state, and district level parties. We also discussed the nature of education and culture in India until it was time for bed.

The next day we went to a local school where I was impressed with all the facilities—science labs with new equipment, the library, the auditorium that doubled as a basketball court, individual desks, and spacious classrooms. I was immediately impressed by the shiny, beautifully designed school building. The classrooms had closed glass windows. Each student had their own chair and desk. In India we had open, wooden windows, and I liked that. Here the students were well-dressed, and everybody had shoes. At my home we were usually barefooted.

The students were very inquisitive and asked thoughtful, intelligent questions about my experiences as a student in India. One of them asked me if we played football. I answered by saying that we call soccer *football* and play with our feet and not hands. Everybody chuckled. At the same time, it made me nostalgic for my childhood school. Even though it was old and crowded, I had many fond memories of it and loved how close you felt to nature with open windows letting fresh air in and the building surrounded with lush fruit trees.

We spent many hours at the school before returning to Mr. Foley's house, where we had dinner, played some ping pong, then again settled down in the living room to talk about our respective lives until about nine o'clock when Mr. Foley drove me back to the hospital. I thanked him for his hospitality and time and watched him drive off. I don't believe I ever saw him again.

Living in India, transportation was never really much of a concern. But it didn't take long to realize that not having a car made life a bit more complicated in the United States. Yes, the East Coast has a lot of public transportation, but the cities are large and heavily populated, so buses, subways, and trains were congested. Cars got you where you were going faster and more directly. I'd been lucky to have so many people willing to drive me from here to there and back.

Like most of us interns, I did not have a car. For one thing I was quite financially constrained because I had to send most of my earnings home to help my family. I believe the salary we were getting was about ninety dollars a month—the equivalent of about $725 in today's money—with free food and lodging. After the hospital deducted taxes and social security, we ended up receiving about seventy dollars. I tried to put some money in the bank, keep some for expenses, and the rest I sent home, so buying a car was out of the question.

For another thing, I did not know how to drive.

Two Indian house officers had bought cars. Dr. Pankhawallah from Bombay—whose wife was also at our hospital—bought a severely bruised, used minivan. The other guy, Jiten, bought a brand-new, red Mustang. They both drove cars in India. He was from the state of Gujarat and quite a flashy fellow. He was also already familiar with American ways because his brother was in the States. I had no idea where he got the money for a new car, but Gujaratis are businesspeople and usually have expertise in managing money.

Buying the car was related to an intimate friendship with a married nurse that he'd begun in the short time he was at the hospital. The nurse's husband left for work early, so she would pick Jiten up, and they'd go back to her house for a morning encounter, which he'd brag about to me. He would describe how they would kiss each other, take their clothes off, lie next to each other, enjoy each other's body, and end the morning by making love. I found his actions unacceptable and had real difficulty understanding why he'd tell me about it. I'm sure the other nurses knew about it too. He ended up buying the Mustang so he could drive himself to her house. The one benefit for me was that I could hitch a ride from him occasionally, and I often accompanied him on weekend road trips.

One day Jiten decided that I should learn how to drive, and I eagerly agreed. Dr. Pankhawallah, who had bought the beat-up minivan, had already taught me some basics. He had me sit in the driver's seat and showed me how to turn the vehicle on and off and explained to me about the steering wheel, brakes, turn signals, windshield wipers, and lights. But he did not let me drive.

Jiten's driving tutoring was more aggressive, in a menacing way. He drove us to a rest stop then we switched seats. After a brief rehearsal of the brakes, accelerator, steering wheel, and turn signals, he instructed me to start the car and drive. He directed me out of the rest stop and directly onto the highway. I objected but he insisted, so someone who had absolutely no idea how to steer a car ended up on the highway. I was not going very fast, so Jiten told me to speed up because I was impeding the cars behind us. But keeping my eyes on the road ahead while staying in my lane and maintaining a higher speed was too much. I just couldn't do it, and I miraculously brought the car to a stop on the shoulder of the highway. We switched seats again, and he drove us back to the hospital.

I was very angry with him for endangering our lives on the highway, and maybe a little annoyed with myself for agreeing. I appreciated him wanting to help me but told him that I needed to learn how to actually drive before going on the highway so I wouldn't kill somebody—or myself. I eventually did learn to drive and took my driving test using Jiten's car. Even though people warned me the test could be difficult, my examiner was very nice, told me I did very well, and I got my license. I had been a little nervous, but it was a breeze. I walked out of the DMV hoping all tests in life were as easy as that one. But when you're a doctor, that's not usually the case.

I went on some memorable rides to many places in Jiten's car. One weekend we were going to Philadelphia. He was driving his new Mustang, and bango, a tractor-trailer hit the car on the passenger side. We pulled over to the side of the road and Jiten was yelling at the truck driver for hitting his car. The truck driver was accusing Jiten of running the red light. Eventually the driver calmed down and requested Jiten not report the accident because he already had a couple of tickets. Nobody was injured. And although there was a massive dent on the passenger side, the car was still drivable, so we resumed our journey.

As we were driving along Jiten told me that he was having difficulty in reading the road signs, traffic signs, and directions while driving. He confessed that he had gone through the red light—which I knew. But I was also amazed at his courage in confronting the truck driver the way he did. It took guts to do that in a new and unfamiliar country.

All the people we visited on our trips were either undergraduate or postgraduate students. Some were research fellows. All lived in small tight quarters. We would spread out, for a night or two, on the floors or sofas. Neither our hosts nor we minded it.

On another occasion Jiten and I were driving back in his repaired Mustang from someplace on a Sunday night. The weather was miserable, and we were somewhat worried. The night was dark, cloudy, and drizzly. We were navigating alright, but the roads were unfamiliar.

Then it started to snow, becoming heavy. I did not have any experience riding in a car in the snow at night. It was probably a first for both of us. To make matters worse, Jiten said the car was almost out of gas. We had to find a gas station. It became a very frightening problem. We were off the highway, driving through small towns. The stores were closed, and more snow was accumulating on the road. The snow-covered streetlights seemed dim, compromising the orientation of the surroundings. The street signs, covered in snow, were difficult to read. We had a roadmap, but the poor visibility made it difficult to follow and we made an occasional wrong turn. It was getting late, our gas was dwindling down, and there was no open gas station in sight. But we kept our patience and did not lose our cool. We kept supporting and encouraging each other.

Out of the corner of my eye, I thought I saw a sign for

a gas station. The lights on the sign looked bright, and big, so I suggested that we go toward the sign. Jiten was reluctant because we had gone to so many gas stations and found them closed. But our gas tank was almost empty, and I was afraid that we'd be stranded in the snow and have to spend the night in the car. Jiten agreed, and we proceeded toward the gas station.

We hit a gold mine. The gas station was open. We were overjoyed with big smiles. There was a nice, older man pumping gas who filled up our tank, and gave us directions to the hospital, saying it was not too far away. Like a father he advised us to stay out of the weather and to drive carefully.

We finally reached the hospital, parked the car, and trudged through the slippery snow to our rooms. It would have been a time for a stiff drink, but we were still Indian and drank the Indian drink—water. We were so relieved, and I congratulated Jiten for bringing us home through those hazardous driving conditions.

I had just walked into my room after finishing my shift when the phone rang. It was the operator who asked me to call the labor room; apparently, I was on call for delivery duty. That was an unexpected bombshell because nobody had told me, and I had no experience delivering babies.

I requested the charge nurse to call the attending. I hesitated to do the delivery.

The nurse ignored my self-doubt. "The attending just left. He was with this patient all day. She wasn't dilating, and he expected the labor was going to be a long one."

Clearly he was wrong.

The nurse then informed me, "The attending is coming back, but he is at least forty-five minutes away. We're holding her cross-legged to prevent the delivery, so you have to come right away."

It was a short distance from our quarters to the hospital and walking over I went over my minimal experience in delivering babies, which was only in medical school. As a student we had to deliver ten babies. For whatever reason most babies were delivered at night. We'd wait in a room fitted with glaring 1000-watt lights intended to keep us awake so we wouldn't miss the delivery. There was also a loud horn that sounded when a delivery was imminent. It was plain torture.

The nursing students had their own stipulated number of deliveries, so we also had to compete with the nursing students for the same deliveries. To make the delivery count, we had to be present from the very beginning, so as soon as the horn sounded, we would run the short distance to the delivery room. But there was a problem. The charge nurse would tip the student nurses off before they would ring the bell to give them a leg up, so we'd often miss the delivery because of that.

Usually deliveries ended up with happy, joyous parents. But not always. I remember one young mother who came from a distant village and was in the late stage of labor. It was about eight in the morning and the registrar, who was like a chief resident, took her to the delivery room. An exam showed there was no amniotic fluid, and the registrar concluded the baby was breech, meaning the buttocks were presenting instead of the head. That is usually a difficult delivery because the baby needs to be turned or will require a caesarian section.

Then the registrar found out that it was not a breech birth but a prolapsed hand, meaning the hand was coming out first. He tried to push the hand back because the patient would immediately need a C-section. This was an enormously difficult situation. It was even more difficult as there was no amniotic fluid.

While the operating room was getting prepared, the professor arrived, and he was furious at how the registrar had handled the case. He chastised him for not recognizing the presentation and wasting valuable time. By the time they went to the OR, neither the mother nor the baby was doing well, and neither survived. Such an awful tragedy. From that point on I wanted nothing to do with obstetrics. But there I was in Connecticut running to another delivery room.

When I arrived, the expert nurse was positioning the patient for delivery. I immediately asked the nurse to call the house officer who was rotating in OB. She told me that I was starting.

The patient was a twenty-three-year-old single mom. This was her first pregnancy, and she was howling with labor pains. The IV drip was going. The monitor was beeping. Gloved and gowned, I sat down on the stool in between the patient's raised legs, and immediately the baby's head came out. I held the head expecting the rest of the body to come out right after. Nothing doing; the baby seemed stuck head out, body in.

I asked the nurse again to please call the last intern on call; she told me he'd been sent for. Sitting there I remembered reading about shoulder dystocia while in medical school, which basically means the shoulders get stuck, often because the baby is proportionately too big for the birth canal. Normally after the head comes out, the shoulder rotates inside the womb to be in line with the birth canal passage then comes out. This process is called restitution.

I tried to rotate the shoulder from outside, and the experienced nurses were trying to put pressure on the shoulder and hyperflex the legs to help me but to no avail. The baby's face was becoming blue, meaning it was asphyxiating. The intern rushed in still wearing his civilian clothes and was not much help. With everybody around me, the patient yelling, and the baby blue, it was tumultuous. Then with the next contraction the baby suddenly came out with great force and dropped in my lap.

With profound relief I clamped the cord, divided it and handed the baby over to the nurse. I delivered the placenta next with no further problem. The baby and the mother were fine, and everybody was happy at the outcome. The attending finally arrived and took over the case. I stayed to help him. It was a nerve-racking experience.

That night when I came out of the hospital, snowflakes were falling gently from the sky, hitting my face, my ears, hair, and the skin of exposed arms. It was my first physical encounter with snow, and I tried to catch the flakes in my hands and on my tongue as I walked back to my room. Even though it was somewhat cold, I was enjoying this beautiful night and embraced the snow as it fell silently from the sky. That first, sweet brush with snow was delightful, especially when compared to my terrifying drive with Jiten in the snow.

Once inside I watched from my window as snow covered the grass, the trees, and the roads in white. Snowflakes danced elegantly in passing car headlights. The next morning everything was still covered with snow, giving everything a different shape when draped in all white. I wrote home to share the experience of my first snowfall but am not sure I had the words to convey its almost magical quality, like a welcome blanket for the new life I'd delivered.

My rotation through OB was colorful, and most of the deliveries were complicated. Sometimes I was the only one to handle the complication, but the nurses were great. The most poignant case for me was a thirteen-year-old pregnant girl, Mary, who I saw as an outpatient. I could not believe that such a young girl was having a baby. Through my entire time in my medical school and short time practicing in India, I had never come across such a situation. There was no dating. Boys and girls were schooled separately. We did not mix with girls. And a young teenage girl would be so protected by her family that it would be extremely difficult for her to get in that situation. Her parents had sent Mary to stay with her grandmother, whether to keep the neighbors from knowing or because they were estranged, I didn't know. But she seemed so alone.

When I finally finished my OB rotation, I was relieved and ready to move on.

The patients in the Griffin hospital's pediatric ward were not acutely sick the way many of my young patients in Calcutta had been. But I was shocked by one stark difference. In my pediatric rotation I witnessed a circumcision, which probably affected me more than the baby. The nurse got the infant and instruments ready for the pediatrician who would do the circumcision. A ball-shaped clamp was placed between the foreskin and the head of the penis. The clamp was tightened, prompting a loud cry from the baby. The instrument was removed, and the foreskin was excised without administering any anesthesia.

I was flabbergasted and horrified to see babies subjected to such a—in my view—barbaric procedure, necessary or not. That said, the babies did very well. Still, it was an eye-opener. Hindus do not circumcise unless it's medically necessary. However, it did not matter what I thought; it was routine and culturally accepted. Despite that cultural disconnect, I enjoyed the pediatric rotation overall. I had pleasant relationships with the nurses and pediatricians as well as with the patients and their families.

At the Griffin, the pediatricians were very good. But as anywhere, there can always be a problem. One of the pediatricians, an excellent one, referred a broken arm case to an orthopedic surgeon, who put the young boy's arm in a cast that was probably too tight. The boy developed a serious circulation problem and was transferred to the Yale New Haven hospital. There was a big to-do about this case and lots of blame went around. I do not know how the boy made out.

Each rotation taught me something new and brought more hands-on experience. On one hand it seemed as if I'd been away from home for a long time, on the other my time at the hospital seemed to be going by so quickly. I'd already been there almost six months. While my professors in medical school back home had been very good, the American system of training and teaching was simply better, especially its use of visual aids.

For example, the hospital didn't have a rotation for pathology, but we'd meet once a week with a pathologist, who would project slides while describing the minutiae of cell structure, and we would understand it much better. By showing as well as telling, I could learn fundamentals easier and quicker. with clearer understanding. Even though I wasn't going to be a pathologist, I learned things that made me a better physician, so I kept up with the readings and was able to answer the pathologist's difficult questions that others could not. It wasn't that I was better than them; they simply chose to neglect studying because they thought his lectures were irrelevant to the subspecialties they were going to choose. They didn't realize that no knowledge ever goes to waste, and I was never more grateful to my parents for instilling that love of learning in me.

Merry and Bright... and Surreal

Thanksgiving had come and gone and now all the nurses were talking about Christmas. That would be another new experience for me, although part of that celebration was familiar. In one area of Calcutta, mostly on Park Street and Chowringhee Road, stores would draw pictures of an old man dressed in red with a white beard and wearing a funny looking cap on their glass windows. There were also pictures of what looked like white stars along with other decorations. Once in America I realized those were depictions of Santa Claus and snowflakes, so obviously there were people in Calcutta who celebrated the Christmas season.

Starting in early December I saw small Christmas trees appear in the nurses' stations, decorated with ornaments and tinsel. There were also multitudes of nuts, chocolates, and other goodies set out in festive trays. All the hospital floors were well decorated with flowers, colored lights, and red-leafed plants I learned were called poinsettias. And different songs started playing, which the nurses called Christmas carols. I really enjoyed them, especially "Jingle Bells." I found myself humming along whenever it played, mostly because other than the *jingle bells*, I couldn't understand most of the other words.

One day I was sitting at the desk when a nurse asked me to stand under a twig hanging from the ceiling. It looked like a little branch with leaves, had a red ribbon around it with a gold bell hanging from it. As I stood there nurses came by and kissed me. I was baffled—and embarrassed—because it was so far outside of my cultural background. Everybody was affectionately teasing me because of my shy reaction.

One of the nurses smiled, "You're standing under mistletoe."

I looked up at the small branch. "I do not see any toes."

That made everyone laugh and then they explained to me what mistletoe was about. My embarrassment quickly passed, and I found it a fun tradition. It was a pleasant encounter. I did a little research on mistletoe and learned that in pre-Christian times the berries of the tree were regarded as symbols of male fertility. In old Greek and Druidic mythology, mistletoe was used as an arrow. Romans hung mistletoe over the doorway to protect the household and associated the plant with love and understanding.

By the eighteenth century, mistletoe had become incorporated with Christmas celebrations around the world. According to tradition, a man was allowed to kiss any woman who stood beneath mistletoe; refusing to kiss brought bad luck for the woman. But now anyone was fair game.

Many homeowners near the hospital decorated their houses for the holiday. The trees, homes, and bushes looked so pretty illuminated by colored lights. It really did create a holiday atmosphere that was contagious. As it got closer to Christmas, the more people talked about shopping, wrapping presents, and the hospital holiday party. Even though I was on call that night, everybody insisted that I and other house officers come to the party since it was on the hospital grounds.

I was really a little nervous about the party. As usual I was worried about the etiquette, what to wear, and the social norms of the party. But I wanted to see what it was like, so after my shift at the hospital, I went to the party still dressed in my white uniform. I was warmly welcomed, and nobody paid any attention to my uniform. But I was a little awestruck seeing everyone all dressed up and dancing to the music playing. They were all in great spirits; the drinks no doubt helped. There was also a lot of food provided.

Nurses, staff, doctors, and some of the attendings came with their spouses. It seemed as if most of the people there were dancing with abandon. Again, the alcohol probably helped that too. The well-dressed crew, the band playing music, the dancing, the food, the drinks—it was so foreign that it was a bit overwhelming. I was also struck by how there was no distinction between the people at the party, which in a class and caste conscious country like India would not be the case.

For a moment I felt completely out of place and took a seat in one corner of the hall to get acclimated. Even though I knew everybody there, and they kept asking me to join, it took a while to break out of my cultural cloak and typical shyness. But when there was a break in the dancing and people started singing Christmas songs and got to "Jingle Bells," I spontaneously joined in. I still wasn't comfortable enough to dance. Where I came from there was no dating, no mixing with girls my age, and we certainly didn't dance together. So not only had I never danced, but neither had I seen any such thing before, other than in the movies. But seeing it in a movie theater was very different from seeing it firsthand. I enjoyed watching and wished I could join in, but I couldn't. This aggregation of Christmas revelers, the gorgeous people all dressed up, the band, the music, the drinks, the food, and the dancing—this extravaganza was fabulous. Needless to say this was another pleasant, new experience. I truly felt the holiday spirit up close and personal.

For as vivid a memory I have of my first Christmas party, I have no real recollection what I did on New Year's Eve, but I can say with confidence I wasn't one of the revelers. While Christmas has an underlying theme of good will and peace on Earth, New Year's seemed more like a bacchanalia. Perhaps this type of New Year tradition might have been embraced by some segment of Indians, but it wasn't by those in my family's circle.

We welcomed the Bengali New Year—which occurs in April—with fanfare but no party or dancing. We celebrated by visiting friends and family and wishing them happiness for the coming year. Bengali New Year was also a good day for the shopkeepers; their regular customers would come by and pay their outstanding bills. Children, such as those in our family, would accompany their fathers, with the expectation of getting to eat some sweets at the stores. Homeowners would clean house—our version of spring cleaning—to make everything fresh.

While I don't remember how I commemorated my first New Year's in the United States, I do know that by January 1963, I was acutely aware that in a matter of months I would be moving on to the next phase of my training, so I was determined to make the most of the time I had left at the Griffin hospital. But my resolution to *carpe diem* sometimes got bogged down in the less exciting aspects of internship.

The Year Comes to an End

The snow, the cold, and the short days made for a dreary winter, and the days took on a not-so-exciting sameness. The other interns and I were spending more time on the floors, doing rounds with the attendings, examining the patients, and discussing or debating diagnoses. After seven months we had our favorite attendings who were more knowledgeable and better teachers than the others. Some of the attendings were not very academic so we tried to skip their rounds whenever possible using whatever excuses we could come up with.

One of my least favorites was Dr. Ferraro, who had a sour disposition and overly loud voice. Everyone knew when he was on the floor. He had a big practice and often had a lot of patients in the hospital. He made a big production of rounding all of us up and holding a clinic on one of his patients, no doubt trying to impress them and everyone else within hearing distance. These consultations often ended up in arguments because he was usually wrong. At the end of the clinic, we would have a laugh behind his back and discuss strategies to avoid him.

In contrast to the patients I saw in Calcutta, in the United States I encountered many patients with chronic obstructive pulmonary disease, or COPD, which is the medical term used to describe a collection of lung diseases that include emphysema and chronic bronchitis. It's been said that COPD is the leading cause of death on the planet. While I cannot confirm that belief, I do know there is currently no cure for the lung damage caused by COPD, and symptoms continually worsen as the disease progresses. Most of the COPD cases I saw at the Griffin hospital were probably related to cigarette smoking. I was flabbergasted to hear patients tell me that they smoked four or five packs of cigarettes *a day*.

I could not imagine how anyone could smoke that many cigarettes. Back home in India smokers would buy a cigarette or two from the corner store because the proprietor would sell individual cigarettes from a pack and the smoker would light the cigarette from the burning end of a burlap rope. Store owners would keep strips of cigarette cartons next to an open flame kerosene lamp. The smoker would light the strip and use it to light the cigarette. Even today in India the practice of selling one or two cigarettes out of a pack continues. It is not because people can only afford a couple of cigarettes a day but because people do not smoke in front of the elders, which restricted their opportunities. That was probably why we did not see that many COPD patients. Indian patients much more often presented with infectious diseases such as tuberculosis, meningitis, typhoid, and gastroenteritis.

We also had a lot of patients with amebiasis, a kind of dysentery that causes abdominal pain, fever, and diarrhea. It's most common in people who live in tropical areas with poor sanitary conditions. We'd treat it with enteroquinol and with painful emetine injections, which were very effective. Some patients would develop an amoebic liver abscess. There was a ward dedicated to those patients, and my colleagues would go on liver rounds draining the abscesses at the bedside. I never saw an amebiasis patient in Connecticut, but many years later in Boston I encountered a very complicated amebiasis case.

The patient was a Vietnam veteran named John, who was admitted to the hospital suffering from abdominal and rectal pain and fever after having undergone a colonoscopy earlier in the day. John's wife, Karen, a nurse at the hospital, requested that I see her husband. She was very worried about him. When I found him, he could barely walk he was in so much pain. Actually, I found him on the floor, crawling between the beds, from the pain. With a nurse's help we put him in the bed. After examining him I first thought he had a perforated bowel and needed surgery. All the nurses were very concerned.

I called Doctor Penny, John's gastroenterologist, to recommend surgery but he brushed aside my diagnosis. He had recently examined John and believed the pain was most likely caused by residual air from the colonoscopy. I reluctantly agreed to wait until the morning and instructed the nurses to call me if there was any change. I called his wife, Karen, and apprised her of the situation. When I stepped out of the elevator the next morning, I saw one of the nurses standing beside a stretcher. She explained that John was very sick, and that Dr. Penny had requested a CT scan.

I saw John immediately and found he was losing his blood pressure, was confused, and continued to have high temperature. All tests pointed to sepsis. I advised the nurse to forget about the imaging; I was taking John to surgery. I apprised Dr. Penny of the situation, and he agreed. During the surgery I found multiple perforations in different areas of the colon, some from the colonoscopy and some from the disease itself. I removed his entire colon and I had to give him an ileostomy, a surgical opening in the abdominal wall for the small intestine so it can be attached to an ostomy bag to collect waste.

John gradually improved and after his discharge from the hospital, continued his normal life with wit and humor and pursued his data processing business. He was lucky; the amebiasis he had contracted in Vietnam was very much out of the ordinary and he had come critically close to dying. Having had that experience had given me a broader diagnostic palette, which every now and then proved very useful.

As the months went by Samar, Nasir, Sujoy, and I continued to hang out and spend time together when we weren't working. We found each other's company comfortable and familiar, and on weekends we'd cook dinner together. Even though we had all attended different medical schools, we had all arrived in America from Calcutta. We enjoyed preparing Indian food. Samar was a particularly good cook. The hospital provided us open access to its kitchen, and we were allowed to take whatever we needed to cook. Mainly we took chicken, oil, and vegetables. It's unthinkable that a hospital would allow that today. Too much concern over liability.

After stocking up from the hospital kitchen, we'd hitch a ride from anyone willing to drive up to a store selling Indian spices. At that time Indian specialty stores were rare. Now you can find Indian spices at Whole Foods or online at Amazon. But then we had to ferret out specialty stores.

I was not a cook—I am still not—but I could help otherwise, such as cutting the vegetables. The aroma of the cooking would waft through our quarters exciting everybody's taste buds. Anyone who wanted to join us was welcome, but many who sampled our dishes couldn't handle the spiciness. We would eat, shoot the breeze, and share a lot of laughter. The conversation often turned to politics, our families back home, navigating through American society and its etiquette, culture, and restrictions. We would dissect the idiosyncrasies of different doctors and members of the nursing staff, which led to discussions about dating.

None of us knew how to approach a lady to ask her out. Plus, there was the fear that she would say no. And considering most of us—Jiten the philanderer being the exception—didn't have much of a social life outside the hospital, odds are it would be a nurse. It would be so embarrassing having to face her at work after she turned you down.

But then one night Nasir came home to our quarters quite late at night with bombshell news. The rest of us were in the hall chatting before going to bed when Nasir walked in quite happy. Nasir was a shy, quiet guy and did not have a particularly charismatic personality.

Besides positively beaming, he was unusually well-dressed for the night, so we immediately wondered what was going on with him.

I asked him, "Nasir, how come you are coming back so late?"

At first he was evasive, then he finally told us that he'd been on a date to the movies with a policeman's daughter and that it was a very enjoyable night. We were gobsmacked. Never in our dreams would we have thought Nasir would be the first one of us to go out on a proper date. (Jiten didn't go on dates with his paramour nor was it proper in any sense.) He was the most unassuming of the group, so that was a revelation. We all went to bed scratching our heads and wondering when we would find our own lady.

One winter weekend Jiten invited me to go to Poughkeepsie, New York, to visit one of his friends, Naven. Poughkeepsie was the home of Vassar College, one of the so-called Seven Sisters, a consortium officially formed in 1926 of women's colleges—Barnard, Bryn Mawr, Mount Holyoke, Smith, Radcliffe, Vassar, and Wellesley—designed to ease the difficulties women's schools were having in raising sufficient endowment money to maintain the high-quality education they offered women of the early twentieth century.

Vassar was founded in 1861 by a brewer, and a philanthropist named Michael Vassar and was the first degree-granting institution of higher education for women in the United States. It would become coed in 1969, but it was still a woman's college when I accompanied Jiten there, although it already had a close relationship with Yale, which was about an hour down the road.

The evening we got there it was freezing cold with a lot

of snow on the ground, at least knee high. But Poughkeepsie was very picturesque. Naven was very likable, cordial, and warm. Naven lived near Vassar. He took us to his room so we could drop off our overnight bags before going out to eat.

Naven said Friday night was pizza night. I knew about pizza but had never eaten any. I was fervently hoping it would not be a rerun of the Thanksgiving turkey experience. Naven said the pizza place we were going to was popular among students. I was slowly starting to understand the implied social interactions; it was a place to mingle with and meet female students. I was both eager to eat pizza for the first time and curious because I had never experienced co-educational classes in India. And the only women I met at work were nurses and patients.

The pizza place was crowded with young people clamoring in groups; it felt like I was back in my medical school cafeteria. Even though it was loud, it was comfortable and welcoming with a good energy. We were lucky and spotted an open booth that we quickly claimed. I don't remember what kind of pizza I ordered. I simply looked at the menu on the wall and picked one. Even though I wasn't all that much older, looking at the young crowd took me back to my college days, which had been such a different world. We did not have girls at any of our gatherings, we didn't have pizza, and we certainly didn't have alcoholic drinks. And women drinking alcohol? Absolutely not.

Now there I was watching young women drinking beer or cocktails. But I was no longer shocked. By then I understood that having a drink together was an accepted social activity among Americans. And I had come to accept this more liberal, open behavior. I wished we'd had that kind of gathering when I was in college. There was such a sense of camaraderie, friendship, and fun. But of course at my table we were very Indian—only sodas, no alcohol.

When the pizzas arrived I took a piece that was still hot, the cheese stretching like strings. With some trepidation I took a small bite. To my relief it tasted delicious, and I devoured my pizza in no time. It was really an enjoyable outing, and I was happy I had come on this road trip.

The next day Jiten and I said good-bye to Naven and thanked him for his hospitality and the good time he'd shown us. We went to Hyde Park, which was just a few minutes away, and took the hour-long guided tour of Franklin Delano Roosevelt's house. It was very interesting to see some history of the United States in person.

In the spring Jiten and I went to Washington, DC, when the cherry blossoms were in full bloom. It was so picturesque as we strolled along the National Mall, surrounded by majestic monuments, the Washington Monument proudly rising to the sky with the US Capitol at the far end.

We visited the Washington Monument first. George Washington was unanimously elected the first president of the new nation in 1789, serving two terms. He died in 1799. Thirty-four years later the Washington National Monument Society was formed to build a monument to honor one of America's first heroes. But because of a lack of funding, political crises, and the Civil War, construction did not begin until 1876, and it took eight years to complete the 555-foot tall obelisk. The monument was built using stones from different quarries, resulting in its different colors.

We wanted to go to the top of the Washington Monument, but there was a long line for the elevator, so we decided to walk it. How hard could it be? We started climbing, and after a while it felt like the steps would never end. Jiten needed to sit down and rest his legs, so I forged ahead without him. When I finally reached the top, I was gasping for air and thought I was going to die. I was so hot, and the observation area was packed, so I had no choice but to stand in the middle of the crowd until I slowly recovered. The handful of windows were four to five people deep, but I eventually found a spot at one of the windows.

I saw the beautiful sights from the top but could not enjoy it because of the horrendous experience climbing the stairs. I discovered there are 898 steps to the top of the Washington Monument, which took more than twenty minutes to scale.

Years later in 1976 I was not surprised to read that the National Park Service had permanently closed the stairs to visitors because too many people had suffered heart attacks while climbing up or hurt themselves falling when coming down. So not only was climbing the steps horrendous, it had also been death-defying. I was never so happy to get on an elevator as I was descending the Washington Monument.

Next we visited the Lincoln Memorial, built with Greek-inspired architecture and made of sparkling white marble that immediately reflects the nobility of the person. There were thirty-six columns depicting the number of states when he was president. Inside the open-air memorial is the large, contemplative sculpture of Lincoln. The steps of the memorial are wide with an intermittent series of platforms. A famous African-American opera singer, Marian Anderson, performed on those steps to an integrated audience in 1939 after she was denied permission to sing at the Daughters of the American Revolution's Constitution

Hall. Not long after we visited, Martin Luther King gave his famous "I Have a Dream" speech on the steps of the Lincoln Memorial.

From there we proceeded to the Jefferson Memorial, which resembled the Pantheon in Rome. It was surrounded by water and gorgeous blooming cherry blossom trees. The open-air chamber of the white marble structure had a striking dome and a pink marble floor along with a bronze statue of Thomas Jefferson. He was the main author of the Declaration of Independence, which was adopted on July 4, 1776. It is inscribed on one of the walls, including the well-known preamble: "We hold these truths to be self-evident, that all men are created equal, that they are endowed by their Creator with certain unalienable Rights, that among these are Life, Liberty, and the pursuit of Happiness." It was majestic.

I was so impressed with all the beautiful architecture, and the stories behind people and their monuments. Visiting Washington was like opening a history book of America. Our trip was an unforgettable experience.

The weeks were quickly passing, and my internship at the hospital was coming to an end. It was time to start looking for a surgical position at a good hospital. Many of the better-known academic institutions did not reply to my applications. But a hospital in Boston invited me for an interview. I met with the chief resident of the surgical program who gave me a tour of their facilities, and I was very impressed. I had also enjoyed driving through Boston; Jamaica Pond, Harvard Square, the Charles River, it was all so pretty. I decided that if the hospital accepted me, I would go there. They did, so I was to be Boston-bound.

The Griffin hospital had weekly or biweekly grand rounds that all the attendings and house officers went to. For these rounds either an outside speaker was invited to give a talk on a special topic, or an attending would discuss a case. Once a year there would be a clinicopathologic conference, or CPC, where a case was given with history, physical, and laboratory results but not the diagnosis. The presenter had to analyze possible differential diagnoses, explain and interpret the test results, and make the final diagnosis.

The hospital had a tradition of selecting a house officer to discuss a case just before the intern year was finished. The hospital selected me to do the CPC. The pathologist was responsible for selecting the case for discussion, which he found in a leading medical journal. He chose a case with cardiac problems and gave me a copy of the EKG. It would be a challenge because I was not good at EKG interpretation.

I reviewed the case history, the laboratory, X-rays, and the EKGs. I consulted many relevant books and journal articles. When I made my presentation, I discussed the different aspects of the case, rationalized the relevant laboratory results, and interpreted the EKG. Then I gave my final diagnosis.

The chief of medicine was very complimentary, saying he thought I had given an excellent review of the case and then opened the floor for discussion. Many of the attendings asked about my EKG interpretation, which they thought was incorrect. However, they all praised my presentation.

At the end, the chief of medicine said that unfortunately my final diagnosis was wrong because I had incorrectly interpreted the EKG, which was the key to the correct diagnosis. That was more than a little humiliating.

But I was happy that so many attendings congratulated me on giving a very good discussion. I was happy about that. The pathologist told me that my discussion was no less, maybe even better, than the discussion in the journal itself. He seemed sincere and not just trying to make me feel better. Either way, it was very generous on his part.

Over my last days at the hospital, I thanked all the nurses and hospital personnel, who had been so very good to me, especially when I was absolutely green in a new country, by helping me learn the customs and social niceties that are the fabric of American culture. I also met the attendings, thanking them for their teaching, guidance, and preparing me for my next endeavor.

My fellow interns and I were all going in different directions. Nasir was going for ophthalmology, Jiten for pathology, and the Pankhawallas for radiology. For as excited as I was to join the surgical program in Boston, I was sad to leave the home away from home that had provided me shelter, friendship, knowledge, and nurturing, making me a better doctor and a more confident person.

I left Connecticut at the end of June 1963 knowing that my life was now on a new path, one I would have never dared to dream of as a youth. While India would always be my home country, the United States was now my adopted country, and I would remain a man of two cultures.

Epilogue:
A Man of Two Cultures

Boston became more than the next stop of my medical training. It would become my home. While in the surgical program there, I met a nurse named Margaret. Despite the fear of rejection and worries of potential future awkwardness, I asked her out. To my delight she said yes. We are still together, but it would take a while for us to actually marry.

After finishing the surgical program in Boston, I traveled to the UK in 1968 to obtain the Fellowship of the Royal College of Surgeons that you need to practice surgery in India. The examination I had to pass by all accounts was very difficult and would require my complete concentration.

I took an admission at the Post Graduate Institute of Medicine, in Edinburgh, Scotland, for a course and moved into an inexpensive rooming house. To my surprise I found a couple of my friends there by chance. My room had a central heater which took up half of the space, but you could feel the heat only when you sat on it. After living with central air and heating in the States, I had become spoiled. So, when I found an advertisement in the Sunday newspaper for a centrally heated room at a reasonable price in that locale, I went to check it out.

I walked up to the house and knocked on the door. A smiling gray-haired lady opened the door and told me that the room was already rented. It struck me odd that it was only about eight o'clock in the morning and the room was already taken, but I thanked her. As I started to walk away, she told me about an area where they take *your kind*. I thanked her again and after a few steps realized her meaning, and I was shocked. It was biased, discriminatory, and insulting. I had never experienced that in my entire five-year stay in the States, even though there was a lot of discrimination against African Americans.

I kept my room at the boarding house and pursued my studies for the upcoming examination. The fellowship examination had two parts: primary and final. You had to pass the primary before you could take the final. As I was preparing for the primary, I received an early morning call from Kalu, my brother in Calcutta, who informed me that our father was very sick. I told him that I would be coming. It meant missing the examination and having to wait months until it was offered again, but my father was more important than my certification. The examination could wait. I took the next flight home.

My father was sick, and was being treated at home with IVs, nasal tube, and twenty-four hour house officer coverage. He was of the generation who grew up afraid of going to the hospital, believing they would not come back. And the rest of my family acquiesced. I took him to the hospital, he got better, and he came home.

As things were settling down, I visited my friends. I wanted to see Mr. Mitra and his little daughter Anita, but with the passage of time, my memory was vague about his address. I went to the neighborhood, but nobody recognized his name. It felt odd because he was well-known there. I went to the iron foundry where he worked; it was on lock out for months. A couple of guards at the gate did not know who Mr. Mitra was either. In spite of several attempts I just could not locate him. I was very disheartened and anguished. I wondered with melancholy what had happened to Mr. Mitra and his beautiful daughter. I never found out and even today remember the Mitra family with sadness in my heart.

It was time for my return to Scotland. The day I left, my father, fully recovered at least for now, was sitting in the verandah when I came to say good-bye. He looked at me, and I looked at him. And in that parting glance we knew it was the last time we would see each other.

On my return I took both the primary in Dublin and the final in London back-to-back and aced them. After the final I sent a letter to my father with the news that I obtained my FRCS, a not-so-easy accomplishment. I got a letter back from my brother saying that our father had died. He hadn't told me that our father had fallen ill again because he knew I was working toward the fellowship, so I missed his death and his funeral.

Up until his death my father still expected me to move back to India full time after I finished the examination. And that had been my original plan: go to America and make some money, go to Britain and get the surgical fellowship, then return to India. But then I met my wife and that derailed those plans. It's like the saying: man makes plans and God laughs. But it gave me a kind of comfort knowing he died believing his child would return.

I ended up staying in Britain for about two years while

waiting for my visa to go back to the United States where Margaret awaited. The visa finally came through in 1970, and Margaret and I were married in 1971. I took her to our house in Calcutta to meet my mother and siblings. They welcomed her with open arms, and she embraced them in kind. Living in Boston with my wife and children while the rest of my family was half a world away made me a man of two worlds. And there's always been a guilt that's part of my life because of it. Anytime someone in my family got sick, I took the next plane to India. But my magnanimous wife never complained or resisted, always encouraging me to go. While I was always leaving someone behind, at the same time, I was always going home, which makes me twice blessed.

And it all started because a little hospital in America sent me a check for airfare to come spend a year in Connecticut.

▲ Young Dr. Roy

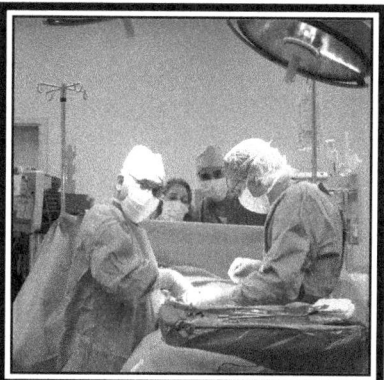

The Operating Room ▲

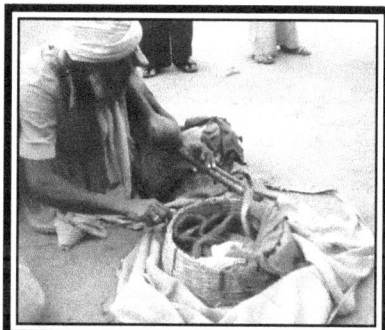

▲ Snakecharmer

▲ Grand Hotel, Calcutta

▲ *Tea Garden*

▲ *Founder of My Medical School*

◀ *On Arrival in USA*

My Childhood Home ▲

About the Author

Dr. Amitabha Ghosh Roy received his MD degree from the Calcutta University, Calcutta, India. He also is a fellow of the Royal College of Surgeons and a fellow of the American College of Surgeons. He was an assistant clinical professor of surgery at Boston University and is an instructor in surgery at Tufts University Medical School. He was the chief of surgery at the Milton Hospital in Milton, Massachusetts, where in 2005 he won the Lira Family Award for Physician Excellence.

An early proponent of Laparoscopic surgery, Dr. Roy held workshops in India and introduced laparoscopic surgery in eastern India. He taught medical students as well as lectured and trained young surgeons both in the United States and in India. Dr. Roy consulted and performed surgery for free during multiple trips to India. He also traveled to Haiti on a medical mission, where he supervised and performed surgery with local surgeons. Dr. Roy also taught Tufts University students in Haiti. Although retired from his general and vascular surgery practice, he continues to participate in the clinical rounds of the hospitals.

In his spare time, Dr. Roy likes to edit home videos to turn them into movies and enjoys photography. He is a Patriots and Red Sox fan and says even though he's the worst golfer, he loves to play.

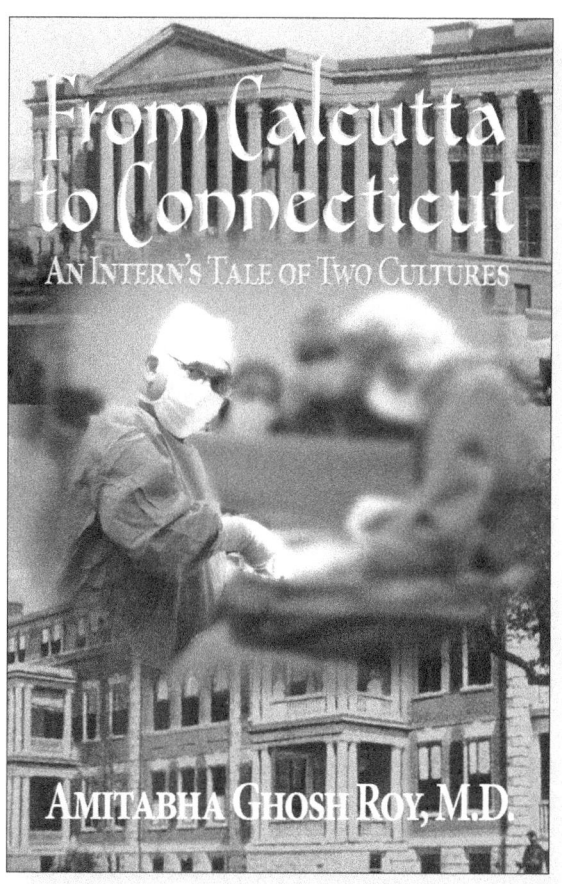

From Calcutta to Connecticut
An Intern's Tale of Two Cultures
AMITABHA GHOSH ROY, M.D.

Publisher: SDP Publishing
Also available in ebook format

www.SDPPublishing.com
Contact us at: info@SDPPublishing.com

CPSIA information can be obtained
at www.ICGtesting.com
Printed in the USA
BVHW040913110621
609355BV00012B/277